RAMBLE

COLORADO

The Wanderer's Guide to the Offbeat, Overlooked, and Outrageous

BY

ERIC PETERSON

ROCK ROLL FOREVER!

speck press

golden

Published by: Speck Press,
An imprint of Fulcrum Publishing
4690 Table Mountain Drive, Suite 100 • Golden, Colorado 80403
800-992-2908 • 303-277-1623 • speckpress.com • fulcrumbooks.com

ISBN13 978-1-933108-19-3

This publication is provided for informational and educational purposes. The information herein contained is true and complete to the best of our knowledge.

Library of Congress Cataloging-in-Publication Data
Peterson, Eric, 1973-
    Ramble Colorado : the wanderer's guide to the offbeat, overlooked, and outrageous / by Eric Peterson.
        p. cm.
    Includes index.
    ISBN 978-1-933108-19-3 (pbk.)
    1.   Colorado--Guidebooks. 2.   Colorado--Description and travel. 3.   Colorado--Miscellanea. 4. Curiosities and wonders--Colorado. 5. Colorado--History, Local. 6. Peterson, Eric, 1973---Travel--Colorado. I. Title.
    F774.3.P47 2008
    917.8804'34--dc22
                                2008000565

Printed in China by Spectrum Books, Inc.

10 9 8 7 6 5 4 3 2 1

Design by Margaret McCullough
Colorado Map provided by Marge Mueller, © Gray Mouse Graphics
Image Credits: pages 4, 12, 47, 89, 139, 163, and the cover © Comstock, pages 9, 38, 45, 86, 109, 110, 115, 118, 122, 123, 128, 141, 142, 146, 161, 162, 171, 173, 179, 181, 199, 201, 202, 203, 209, 210 © Shutterstock, page 214 © iStock, pages 23, 36, 45 © Library of Congress, pages 74, 76 © Jason E. Kaplan, page 17 © Lawrence Argent, page 96 © Gunnison-Crested Butte Tourism Association, page 104 © Jon Barnes, all other photos © Eric Peterson.
For specific information about individual photographs, please contact the publisher.

To Mom.

**Thanks for childbirth,
childhood, life,
and all that good stuff.**

THANKS TO:

Ruthie, Margaret McCullough, Susan Hill Newton, Derek Lawrence,
Pete "Dad" Peterson, Mark Mandarich, Ingvald Grunder, John "Duff" Allen,
Clay "Cash" Kiser and crew, Pampa and Mary, Nick Bohnenkamp,
Roman Bodnar, Don Davidson, Dennis Meeker, Nicky DeFord,
Lauren Pelletreau, Carly Grimes, Scott Stoughton, K. K., Rich Grant
and the Denver Metro CVB, Olivia, Mitch, Sam, Arin, Brad,
3 Kings Tavern, Gennaro's, Johnny Fisher and the Home Ranch,
Emily McCormack, the Limelight Lodge in Aspen,
Lancaster's Western Wear, Casa Bonita, Marty Jones, Dale Katechis,
Kosta Razatos, L. J., Don and Barb Laine, David Lewis,
Kelly Regan, the Sturms, the Ojenneses, the Kromers, and Moose.

DINOSAUR
CITY LIMIT
ELEV 5900 FT
GOVERNOR'S
SMART GROWTH
& DEVELOPMENT
AWARD

CONTENTS

INTRODUCTION

Colorado, a name that conjures images of skiers whizzing down snowy mountains, cowboys smoking cigarettes and branding cattle, and hippie burnouts smoking pot and, uh, whizzing down snowy mountains.

But if you were born here—like I was—then perhaps it might just seem like any other nearly perfect rectangle on the map. Skiers and potheads and mountains and cowboys fade into the woodwork amidst the strip malls and highways and suburbs.

When I take a step back, I realize there *is* something magical about the state. Colorado is one of the most valuable brand names in the union, thanks in large part to those imaginary skiers who slalom through people's brains when they hear the word. Whereas West Virginia and North Dakota struggle to repair or refine their public image, Colorado is a brand that's long been able to sell beer and trucks and smokes and all sorts of other consumer products for a good long time. In the end, however, Colorado is a place, and like any other place, it is not a concept or idea but a tangible thing with its own unique inhabitants, geology, politics, and peculiarities, not to mention history—which is as good a place as any to start.

The rectangle on the map now known as Colorado was home to native people for 13,000 years or so until the Europeans started showing up in the late 1500s. The United States bought the eastern side of modern-day Colorado from France as part of the Louisiana Purchase in 1803 and forced Mexico to give up the rest of it as part of the treaty ending the Mexican-American War in 1848. Three years later, the first European settlers—who also happened to be Hispanic—moved to what is now Colorado and established the town of San Luis.

Most of the state was part of the Territory of Kansas throughout the 1850s, but a gold rush in 1858 led to a few residents trying to establish it as a separate Territory of Jefferson. That plan didn't fly—probably because the Republican-controlled Congress didn't want to honor a Democratic Southerner on the eve of the Civil War—and the area enjoyed a month in limbo after eastern Kansas became a state in January 1861. After a month of anarchy, the

Territory of Colorado was officially established in February. Fifteen years later, only 132 years ago, the Centennial State came into being.

Since then, the three most important moments in Colorado history are the genesis of the state's ski industry, in 1915, the Denver Broncos' first Super Bowl victory, in 1998, and the mania surrounding Crocs-brand footwear in Boulder, in 2002. The first important moment—the opening of Howelsen Hill in Steamboat Springs—needs no explanation. The second helped give the state confidence on the national stage, which wavered after the Broncos, worshipped with fundamentalist fervor by fans, lost four Super Bowls by a cumulative score of 163 to 50. The third and final important moment cemented the fact that Coloradans can out-casual any other state by wearing candy-colored polymer clogs instead of tying our shoes.

Beyond the slopes and the pro football team and the neon footwear, what I ultimately love about Colorado are the vast tracts of wilderness and open space, the amazing spots around so many bends in the road, and the location pretty much in the middle of nowhere, which is exactly where I want to be.

—*Eric Peterson*

DENVER AND THE FRONT RANGE

INTRODUCTION

Sandwiched between the mountains and the plains are the vast majority of Colorado's people. The Front Range is most likely the state's population center because of the laziness of westbound pioneers who saw the ominous silhouette of the Rocky Mountains on the horizon and said, "I don't know about California, but this place looks okay to me."

The population and suburban sprawl along Colorado's Front Range have accumulated more or less continuously ever since those first gold junkies set up camp on the banks of the Platte River. Now the region—stretching from Pueblo to Fort Collins—is home to nearly 80 percent of the state's residents, most of them living in metro Denver.

Alternately known as the Mile High City and the Queen City of the Plains and Cowtown, Denver was named for James Denver, the Kansas governor who'd quit before the moniker was bestowed, ironic because the hope was he would grant political favors to the town that bore his name. While James Denver is buried in the history books, John Denver remains well known, another irony inasmuch as the man who took

STATS & FACTS

- The U.S. Mint in Denver opened in 1906 and struck 167 million coins during its first year in operation. A century later, the facility made that many coins in a week—or 8 billion a year.

- Zebulon Pike "discovered" 14,115-foot Pikes Peak in 1806, but he never made it to the top. Today an estimated 10,000 hikers summit the mountain annually.

- Thanks to its now-closed dynamite factory—and the occasional DuPont truck filled with nitroglycerin crossing the town's railroad tracks—Louviers, a small town south of Denver, earned the somewhat satanic nickname of "Hellsville."

- In 1953, the Denver sheriff's department asked Frank Marugg, an inventor and violinist with the Denver symphony, for help with parking enforcement. Marugg tinkered around and came up with a device to immobilize cars whose owners failed to pay their tickets, a clamp that came to be known as the "Denver Boot."

- Before Cherry Creek Reservoir, there was Castlewood Canyon Reservoir. Now in ruins, its dam—labeled unbreakable by its builders in 1890—indeed broke in 1933, sending a twenty-foot wave straight into downtown Denver.

his name from the city has done better in the fame game than the guy from whom the city took its name. (Bob Denver [Gilligan] places second in Denver's "most famous" race.)

Regardless of its origins, the name *Denver* brings to mind images of mountains and cowboys to Easterners, rather than a city complete with graffiti, pollution, and crack. This isn't to say that urban decay has totally sublimated Denver's Western charms—it's only partially sublimated them; a fascinating contrast, in my humble opinion.

South of Denver, Colorado Springs is the state's second biggest city and known mostly as a bastion of conservative Christians, soldiers, and tech geeks. Northward are the college towns of Boulder and Fort Collins, known for more-progressive politics, occasional drunken riots, and higher, um, education.

BIG THINGS AND OTHER ROAD ART

Swetsville Zoo
Just east of I-25, exit 265
4801 E. Harmony Rd., Timnath
970-484-9509

Bill Swets is a farmer by trade, an artist at heart, and a tinkerer above all. His eponymous city-zoo is populated with spiders, dinosaurs, dragons, and all sorts of other critters made of junk: car parts, agricultural implements, discarded sheet metal, etc. Today the zoo is home to about 150 metal beasties, not to mention an old boat and a sporadically open tenant gallery. A life's work with farm machinery robbed Bill of his hearing, but he reads lips pretty well...enough to tell you what you need to know about the Swetsville Zoo.

Read:

- On the Road by Jack Kerouac, The First Third by Neal Cassady, Modern Drunkard magazine

Listen:

- Anyone labeled as part of the "Denver sound," most notably Slim Cessna's Auto Club and Munly

View:

- WarGames, Mork and Mindy, Dynasty, Every Which Way But Loose

To-Do Checklist:

- Enjoy a Denver omelet (or a Denver Boot, if you're vegetarian)

- Have a local beer or three

- Join the Mile High Club (anywhere except the steps of the Capitol building)

Denver Art Museum
100 W. 14th Pkwy., Denver
720-865-5000
www.denverartmuseum.org

An abstract titanium-skinned spaceship landed in central Denver in 2006…no wait, that's the new avant-garde addition to the Denver Art Museum. Instantly the most distinctively weird building in town, the Daniel Libeskind–designed structure is an odd contrast with the older building: a seven-story castle clad in exactly one million grey tiles. Oh, and there is plenty of good art inside and out, the latter including *The Yearling*, a sculpture of a normal-sized horse on a twentyfive-foot-tall chair by Donald Lipski, and *The Big Sweep*, an enormous broom and dustpan by big-things specialists Claes Oldenburg and Coosje van Bruggen.

ZaBeast

Forney Museum of Transportation
4303 Brighton Blvd., Denver
303-297-1113
www.forneymuseum.org

After starting with stickers from his son's sports teams a decade ago, Al Pallone gradually enveloped his 1975 Pontiac Grandview in adhesive propaganda for heavy metal bands, cartoon characters, and pretty much everything else. After *ZaBeast* accumulated 5,000 stickers—not to mention the action figures populating the hood and dash, and the fake gorilla mitts hanging from the trunk—the service life of Colorado's first art car ended in 1997 when the engine blew. Pallone donated it to the Forney Museum of Transportation, where it has been on display ever since alongside Amelia Earhart's *Gold Bug* and the Porsche from *Risky Business*.

Big Blue Bear

Colorado Convention Center
Corner of 14th St. and
California St., Denver

Peering into the Colorado Convention Center, the Lawrence Argent sculpture *I see what you mean* is a forty-foot-tall blue bear that instantly became the Mile High City's most lovable piece of public art when it was installed in 2005. Argent, a working artist and art professor at the University of Denver, is the mastermind behind a number of other eye-grabbing works of public art in metro

Denver, including *Ghost Trolley* at Colfax Avenue and Elmira Street in Aurora and *Virere,* the twenty-foot aluminum blades of grass at the corner of Broadway and Yale in Englewood. And if you really can't get enough of the big blue bear, Argent commissioned two miniature scale models to sell as souvenirs, available at both the convention center and the gift shop at the Denver Art Museum.

Pueblo Levee Mural Project: World's Longest Painting
Along the Arkansas River levee, Pueblo

The levee holding back the Arkansas River for more than three miles as it passes through Pueblo is a concrete canvas for what the Guinness folks have certified as the world's longest painting. What began as oddball paintings by the anonymous and nocturnal Tee Hee Artists in the late 1970s soon became legitimized by a community-approved organization that upped the artistic ante. Since then, scores of local artists have slowly covered two miles (and counting) of continuous levee with vibrant artwork depicting everything from pro-recycling logos to Aztec history to Elvis Presley.

Tiny Town
Off U.S. 285, 6249 S. Turkey Creek Rd., near Morrison
303-697-6829
www.tinytownrailroad.com

So far there never has been a *King Kong in the Old West* movie. But if there ever is, Tiny Town would make a solid location. The owner of a moving company, George Turner built a one-sixth-scale model of a Western town for his daughter in 1915 and opened it to the public in 1920. Ravaged by the elements, Tiny Town was on the verge of becoming Tiny Ghetto in the 1980s, and so a local group formed to fix it up (including the miniature railroad), maintain it, and build more tiny structures, including several storefront-lined city blocks, a Dr. Seuss–style house, and a one-sixth-scale Coney Island hot dog stand, a tribute to the real thing in Bailey.

Alice in Wonderland Statues
Greenwood Plaza, outside of Coors Amphitheatre, 6350 S. Greenwood Plaza Blvd., Greenwood Village
303-806-0444
www.moaonline.org

Part of the south suburban Museum of Outdoor Art's collection, a ring of captivating *Alice* bronzes by Harry Marinsky dot the sidewalks surrounding the outdoor music venue known as Coors Amphitheatre. Beyond Alice, there is the White Rabbit, the Mad Tea Party, the Cheshire Cat, the Caterpillar smoking his hookah on a mushroom, and a ferocious Queen of Hearts. For *Alice* fans, it's worth the wander in the 'burbs.

Benson Sculpture Park
29th St. and Beech Dr., Loveland

A chunk of forested land with an alligator, wolves, and a two-ton gorilla might sound like a scary place, but it is actually the opposite: a park that doubles as an outdoor gallery featuring 100 sculptures on permanent display. On a one-mile stroll, you can spot both naked people and children sledding, anytime of year.

Starr Kempf's Kinetic Sculptures
2057 Pine Grove Rd. (at Evans Ave.), Colorado Springs

Artistic genius of staggering proportions, the late Starr Kempf is well known in Colorado Springs for his whimsical wind-powered kinetic sculptures. Remarkable feats of engineering,

his steel sculptures spin, twist, and otherwise move with the breeze. The front yard of his former home and studio in Cheyenne Cañon is the best place to see his work. But don't dawdle: The tyrannical powers that be once ordered them off the property because of zoning issues. But only three were removed, so a good number remain. These metallic master-pieces make up one of the most amazing outdoor galleries in the state, and should stay right where they are.

Giant Hercules Beetle

CO 115 and Rock Creek Canyon Rd.
at the May Museum entrance,
8 miles south of Colorado Springs

Strangely enough, the world's largest roadside replica of the world's largest beetle is at the foot of the Rockies, not in a tropi-cal habitat where the real things live. Found in North, Central, and South America, these impressive insects max out at seven inches in length. This one, however, is a full sixteen feet long. We can only be happy that the real things are not this size.

R.I.P.

Alfred (a.k.a. Alferd) Packer, 1842–1907

Littleton Cemetery
Under the tree near the second-most northern entrance
6155 S. Prince St., Littleton

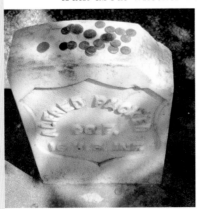

Colorado's favorite illiterate cannibal ate the other four members of his gold-rushing party from Provo, Utah. The truth about whether he killed them or not—he claimed he only defended himself from the true killer, then ate the carnage to survive—went with him to his grave in Littleton Cemetery. After his original confession, in 1874, Packer (known as both Alfred and Alferd because of his own illiteracy) spent nearly a decade on the lam before being apprehended living under an alias in Cheyenne, Wyoming. However, his second incarceration was again cut short. After a news-paper reporter convinced the gov-ernor to commute Packer's forty-year sentence in 1901, he was paroled and lived out his remaining days in the Denver foothills (understandably) as a vegetarian.

Neal Cassady Sr., 1893–1963

Mount Olivet Cemetery
Unmarked gravesite south of Maria Lopez's grave
Section 26, Block 5, Lot 6, Grave 9
12801 W. 44th Ave., Wheat Ridge

One of the best-known drunken bums of all time, Neal Cassady Sr.'s fame stems entirely from that of his son, a wandering nomad who shared some his father's indigent alcoholic inclinations. As inspiration for Dean Moriarty in Kerouac's *On the Road*, Neal Cassady Jr. described his father as a bum on Larimer Street. While the Larimer of both Cassadys has for the most part disappeared, the gravesite of the father—now in the shadows of an I-70 overpass—is an anonymous reminder of the anonymous crossroads Denver used to be.

Buffalo Bill, 1846–1917

Cedar Mountain, Cody, WY
Or (depending on who you believe) Lookout Mountain,
987½ Lookout Mountain Rd., Golden
www.buffalobill.org

William "Buffalo Bill" Cody was the architect of the popularized mass-media view of the West, and his fingerprints are all over popular culture to this day. Late in his career, Cody signed a bad contract, lost most of his fortune, and died in Denver in 1917. That's where the intrigue begins.

The Denver Post and the city of Denver allegedly bribed Cody's sister to keep his body in Colorado. But he died in January, with frost gripping Lookout Mountain, where Denver leaders wanted to bury him based on what his sister said were his wishes. So the powers that be put "Buffalo Bill" on ice until the summer.

A few months later, an anonymous old cowboy died in Cody, Wyoming. Cody locals insisted Founding Father William Cody wanted to be buried on Cedar Mountain, outside of town. So a trio of interlopers trimmed the dead cowboy's beard and transported him down to Denver, where they proceeded to requisition the necessary key, swap bodies, and take the real deal back to the city that bears his name.

Cody's descendents are reputed to believe his final resting spot to be on Cedar Mountain in Wyoming and not

Lookout Mountain in Colorado, where the Colorado National Guard once guarded the grave in the 1940s (purportedly as a publicity stunt), well after the Mile High posse sealed the deal with several tons of concrete in 1927.

Dean Reed, 1938–1986

Green Mountain Cemetery
Near the back center of section K
290 20th St., Boulder
303-444-5695

After his attempt at pop stardom fizzled in the U.S., musician and actor Dean Reed fostered a South American fan base, moved to Argentina, and became a leftist activist against his native country's foreign policy. Argentina deported him in 1966, and he eventually landed in East Germany, where he emerged as the Soviet Union's biggest musical sensation. Despite his outspoken opposition to U.S. policy—which attracted a lot of hate mail and death threats—Reed never renounced his U.S. citizenship, and he filed tax returns with the I.R.S. until his mysterious drowning in 1986, which some say was murder and others claim was suicide.

Linda Lovelace, 1949–2002
Parker Cemetery
10735 S. Parker Rd., Parker

Born Linda Susan Boreman, Lovelace became an international star after *Deep Throat* made "porn" and "blow job" household words. The film pulled in $600 million gross, however Lovelace maintained that she was never paid a penny for her role. In the 1980s, she campaigned against the evils of pornography and released her autobiography *Ordeal*, which describes how her husband forced her into porn at gunpoint, among other things.

VICE

El Chapultepec
1962 Market St., Denver
303-295-9126

One of the only old-school spots in LoDo to survive the post–Coors Field boom, El Chapultepec is the best jazz club for hundreds of miles. Open since Prohibition ended in 1933, the claustrophobic, checkerboard-floored nightspot morphed from derelict dive to music venue in the early 1950s. In the time since, the stage has been taken by such music legends as Frank Sinatra, Ella Fitzgerald, and Keith Richards (usually after big-arena concerts in town), and it continues to attract world-class talent. And the burritos aren't bad either.

DEAR DEPARTED DOGS

Not too surprisingly, canine-loving Colorado has a quartet of graves and memorials for famous dogs of the Front Range.

Annie, 1934–1948
C&S Depot
201 Peterson St., Fort Collins

Railroad workers discovered Annie, sick and pregnant, in a blacksmithing shop in nearby Timnath and brought her to the depot where she had her litter and rested back to health. Annie then adopted the depot as home and barked greetings at every arriving train for the next fourteen years.

Yogi, 1989–1998
Aurora Police K-9 Cemetery
Deborah Sue Corr Police Training Center
behind the Beck Recreation Center
800 Telluride St., Aurora

Yogi is a legend in the missing-persons business, thanks to a truly super-canine sense of smell. With partner Officer Jerry Nichols, this bloodhound worked hundreds of cases for seventy different law enforcement agencies, winning numerous

medals and awards and once tracking a missing child for four days and fourteen miles—and the case was an automobile abduction. Generally credited with having the best nose on any dog ever, Yogi worked tirelessly and passed away a mere month after his last day on the job.

Shep, 1950–1964
U.S. 36, just southeast of U.S. 287
Colorado 121/Wadsworth Blvd., Broomfield

When the Boulder Turnpike (a.k.a. U.S. 36) was under construction in the early 1950s, Shep arrived as a stray puppy at a work site. Thanks to the workers sharing their lunches, the tollbooth operators who followed found Shep had made himself at home. The mutt became locally famous and was even adopted as the unofficial mascot of the Colorado Department of Transportation. Now Shep's twin memorial markers—"Our Pal" and "Part Shepherd, Mostly Affection"—sit  on a patch of weeds tucked on the southeast corner of the Wadsworth overpass, near where the long-gone tollbooth once operated. It's a bit of a hike down from the nearby commuter parking lot, but someone often makes the trip, because fresh American flags regularly arrive at the memorial.

Dizzy, (birth and death dates unknown) circa 1930–1940
In front of Town Hall, Palmer Lake

Named after Hall of Fame pitcher Dizzy Dean, this German shepherd carried the necessary light bulbs, wire, and tools up Sundance Mountain for the very first Palmer Lake Star to mark the 1935 winter holiday season. Visible from I-25 every December, the star is a local tradition first made possible by Dizzy's hard work hauling gear up the mountain's 60 percent grade in dog-sized saddlebags.

Cruise Room
Oxford Hotel, 1600 17th St., Denver
303-825-1107

Swathed in dim red light, the Cruise Room oozes swank and cool. Opened the day after Prohibition ended in 1933, this bar off of the lobby of the Oxford Hotel in LoDo was modeled after a lounge on the *Queen Mary* ocean liner, its Art Deco panels depicting drinking toasts from different cultures and its bar staff the most capable martini makers in town.

My Brother's Bar
2376 15th St., Denver
303-455-9991

Said to be Denver's oldest surviving watering hole—although not continuously operated as one—My Brother's Bar is best known for three key distinctions: its grand opening in 1873; its status as a Beat landmark because a young Neal Cassady drank here; and its expertly grilled burgers, delivered with a Plexiglas cabinet full of fixings.

PT's Showclub

1601 W. Evans Ave., Denver
303-934-9135
www.ptsshowclub.com

This strip club in a vaguely industrial area in southwest Denver has had quite a storied history. In the late 1960s, the space was home to a music venue called the Family Dog and hosted the Grateful Dead, Janis Joplin, Jimi Hendrix, and The Doors during the summer of love, or soon thereafter. In the 1970s, it became a topless club named PT's, in honor of P. T. Barnum, and is said to be the first multiple-stage strip club in the world. Today it's still a strip club and most notable for its somewhat unsettling coed weekend nights that attract swingers and bachelorette parties and allow male amateurs to doff their duds on one stage while female pros work the crowd.

Stranahan's Colorado Whiskey

2405 Blake St., Denver
303-296-7440
www.stranahans.com

Jess Graber and George Stranahan, the owner of Denver-based Flying Dog Brewery, met under unfortunate circumstances: in the afterglow of a blaze that claimed a barn on Stranahan's Pitkin County ranch. That barn was history, but Stranahan had "another barn with running water and a warm space," said Graber. "In Colorado, you need that." There they distilled a couple of leftover kegs, and the results spurred them to launch a full-fledged operation that used barley mash from Flying Dog. The whiskey is aged in charred white-oak barrels for no less than two years (the first batch debuted in April 2006) and cut with pure spring water to make a spicy 94-proof blend.

Bud's Bar

5453 Manhart St. (just west of U.S. 85), Sedalia
303-688-9967

What *was* Herman's Garage became Bud's Bar in 1948, when Bud Hebert went into the libation business. (I'm not sure what happened to Herman.) About a dozen years later, Bud got a job as a Douglas County judge, so he legally couldn't own a bar. He sold it, but his name stuck through the years. The place is known for cold beer and burgers. In fact, the menu has just four options—hamburgers, double hamburgers, cheeseburgers, and double cheeseburgers—and "No Fries, Dammit!" Chips. No Coke, either. Pepsi.

3 Kings Tavern

60 S. Broadway Ave., Denver
303-777-7370
www.3kingstavern.net

This rock club in the heart of the hip Baker District is decorated like the id of an eternal teenager, with a hallway wallpapered in comic books and a veritable gallery of rock memorabilia and kitsch on the walls and in a display case. Local and touring bands play loud music here most nights of the week.

Rocky Flats Lounge

11229 S. CO 93, about 10 miles north of Golden
303-449-4242

Located in the windswept middle of nowhere between Golden and Boulder, the Rocky Flats Lounge is the consummate roadhouse, with a woodsy, slightly ornery vibe and loads of character. A payroll-office-turned-watering-hole for employees of the nearby Rocky Flats Plant, a nuclear weapons facility that was shuttered due to safety violations and the ensuing controversy, the lounge nowadays attracts mostly blue-collar types, namely bikers, and fans of the Green Bay Packers. But it still plays off its toxic heritage in its T-shirts: "I got nuclear wasted at the Rocky Flats Lounge."

Buckhorn Exchange
1000 Osage St., Denver
303-534-9505
www.buckhorn.com

Not only is the Buckhorn Exchange the oldest restaurant in the Mile High City, it's also the proud owner of Colorado Liquor License No. 1, issued when Prohibition ended in 1933, and home to the world's first lighted beer sign, an invention of Coors Brewery in nearby Golden.

Redstone Meadery
4700 Pearl St., Unit 2A, Boulder
720-406-1215
www.redstonemeadery.com

Mead, or honey wine, is the oldest fermented beverage on the planet, as alcohol historians theorize that a rain-soaked beehive produced the first accidental batch some 3,000 years ago. Colorado's mead leader is Redstone Meadery in Boulder, which offers free tours and tastings and sells its wares from its east Boulder location. Redstone is also the driving force behind the annual International Mead Festival, held in the People's Republic every February since 2003.

Other Front Range barroom superlatives include: Gennaro's, yours truly's favorite neighborhood bar, at 2598 S. Broadway in Denver (303-722-1044), Sam's the World's Smallest Bar (109.57 square feet), at 22 North Tejon Street in Colorado Springs (719-473-0678), and Gus's Place, at 1201 Elm Street in Pueblo (719-542-0755), once deemed by the *Ripley's Believe It or Not!* people as the national champ for beer sold per square foot.

STAR MAPS

A can't-miss attraction whether there's a show or not, fabled Red Rocks Amphitheatre in Morrison has hosted everyone from Slayer to the Indigo Girls to the Grateful Dead to Ween, but it also hosted the only concert The Beatles did not sell out on their first American tour, in 1964.

The exterior of the place Mork and Mindy shared is 1619 Pine Street in Boulder. Also in *Mork and Mindy*'s opening credit sequence, Mork landed in Chautauqua Park, on the south side of town.

While the Carrington Mansion in the credits is actually in Southern California, prime-time soap *Dynasty* was set in Denver and featured cityscapes and other local sights in the credits.

Led Zeppelin and the Jimi Hendrix Experience played their respective first and last U.S. concerts in Denver.

Star Wars X-Wing
Wings Over the Rockies Air & Space Museum
7711 E. Academy Blvd., #1, Denver
303-460-5360
www.wingsmuseum.org

On permanent loan from Lucasfilm, this German-made three-quarter-scale X-Wing served as a promotion for *Star Wars Episode I: The Phantom Menace* in Tokyo, then migrated across the Atlantic to Denver for a *Star Wars* fan event. The lovingly maintained X-Wing often hits the road for fan events, but it always returns back to its home in the museum's hangar at the former Lowry Air Force Base, where special events attract squadrons of costumed Stormtroopers and Rebels.

HUH?

Downtown Aquarium

700 Water St., Denver
303-561-4450
www.aquariumrestaurants.com

There are few places where aquaphiles can snorkel and dive with sharks in the middle of a major city. There are fewer yet that sit 1,000 miles from the nearest ocean. The odd exception is Denver's Downtown Aquarium. The largest aquarium between Chicago and Monterey, California, this is one of the only such facilities outfitted to allow the public to get up close and personal with its resident fish. In the 300,000-gallon tank, certified divers can drop in on the resident sharks (there are twenty-one members of non-aggressive species like nurse, sand tiger, and zebra sharks) and go eye to eye with a Pacific green sea turtle. Snorkelers can explore the 200,000-gallon "Under the Sea" exhibit, home to more nurse sharks, as well as green moray eels (with mugs that only eel mothers could love) and a whopping 300-pound Queensland grouper.

Cheyenne Mountain and NORAD
On the west side of Colorado Springs
www.norad.mil

Deep inside Cheyenne Mountain on the west side of Colorado Springs is the most Strangelove-ian remnant of the Cold War: the operations center for the North American Aerospace Defense Command (NORAD).

After the Department of Defense pinpointed it as the most defensible spot for a combat operations center in the event of a nuclear war, Cheyenne Mountain was designed to survive the blast from a thirty-megaton bomb landing within a mile. Comprised of fifteen buildings in a massive man-made cavern, the entire facility is under about 2,000 feet of granite. The twenty-five-ton blast doors had their Hollywood moment in *WarGames*, but the movie version of the operations center is nothing like the real thing, which has the feel of a shabby, out-of-date I.T. facility.

In 2006, NORAD's day-to-day operations moved to an ordinary building at nearby Peterson Air Force Base, leaving Cheyenne Mountain on "warm standby." While public tours are no longer available, I'm really hoping the underground operations center will eventually become a national historic site or perhaps a doomsday-themed amusement park. But for the time being, you can visit the surface of Cheyenne Mountain, home to hiking, high-end neighborhoods and resorts, and a zoo.

Frozen Dead Guy
Nederland
www.frozendeadguy.com

Paradoxically, Bredo Morstoel, Nederland's most famous resident, never lived in the town, although he's been there since 1993 and has been celebrated with a festival every March since 2002. Bredo lived in Norway and died there in 1989. At the behest of his grandson Trygve Bauge, his body was packed in dry ice and shipped to California, where he was frozen in liquid nitrogen, in hopes he might one day be revived. Then Trygve, then a Boulder resident, transported Grandpa Bredo to a shed in Nederland, where his coffin was packed in dry ice. Officials with the town of Nederland found out about Bredo in 1994 and made a law against storing frozen dead people in sheds, but Bredo was grandfathered in. While Trygve was deported to Norway, a local "cryogenicist" devotee has kept grandpa securely packed in dry ice, hauling a ton up from Denver every month or so, maintaining that he is merely in suspended animation and will soon snap out of it.

DIA Conspiracy
Denver International Airport, Denver
www.flydenver.com

If you believe what you read on the Internet, Denver International Airport is apparently the future North American HQ for the New World Order, complete with Masonic symbols, allegedly post-apocalyptic murals, and an enormous labyrinth of subterranean tunnels that hide deep, dark secrets about the Illuminati and every shadowy conspiracy in the book. Online theorists note that the Queen of England has been buying up property in the area, that whistleblowers have killed themselves, that Nazi "Black Sun" worship ties heavily into the airport's secrets, and that the mayor of Denver was paid off by the CIA to keep quiet about the whole thing.

The airport is the nation's largest, at more than fifty square miles, and its construction necessitated the relocation of 100 million cubic yards of earth (one-third of that moved for the Panama Canal). Its sheer size, as well as its seemingly illogical location in the middle of nowhere and its since-shuttered robotic luggage system, makes good fuel for the fire. As does the mural with the guy in the gas mask. He's really creepy.

Nikola Tesla's Laboratory
Knob Hill
1 mile east of downtown Colorado Springs

Electricity genius Nikola Tesla, dubbed "the man who invented the twentieth century" by biographer Robert Lomas, relocated from New York to Colorado Springs in 1899. He chose

the then-fledgling mountain town because of its geomagnetic properties and spent the better part of a year there cooking up ground breaking and never-repeated experiments with more and more arcane tech-nology. He created 100-footbolts of lightning—the only man-made lightning in history—and wirelessly transmitted electricity, amazingly lighting bulbs screwed into the ground twenty-six miles away. At one point, he picked up radio signals that he theorized originated on Venus or Mars, but his mad scientist persona turned off potential financiers. Broke, Tesla abandoned his Colorado Springs lab in 1900, and it was torn apart and its contents liquidated to pay off the debts he left behind.

GRUB

Birthplace of the Cheeseburger
2776 Speer Blvd., Denver

Denver is not the only alleged birthplace of the cheeseburger— Pasadena, California, and Louisville, Kentucky, also make the claim—but it *is* the city that went to the trouble of erecting a granite monument to commemorate the landmark culinary event. Louis Ballast, proprietor of the now-defunct Humpty Dumpty Drive-In, tried to trademark the word *cheeseburger* in 1935, and he may have succeeded but he never sued anyone for using his name.

Nevertheless, the bickering over the cheeseburger's origins continues as if the innovation of cheese on a hamburger is akin to atomic fission and not just a major step for the U.S. in its remarkably successful campaign to become the most obese nation in the history of the world.

Fool's Gold Loaf

The year 1976 saw Elvis Presley and his entourage jet to Denver to gorge on the house specialty at a since-shuttered restaurant called the Colorado Gold Mine Company. The King's beloved delicacy: the $50 Fool's Gold Loaf, a slab of a sandwich consisting of a buttered, browned, and hollowed-out loaf of Italian bread stuffed with the unholy trinity of peanut butter, jelly, and bacon. Elvis allegedly consumed one loaf himself (estimated calories: 3,000 for a jar of peanut butter plus 1,250 for the jam plus 2,500 for a pound of bacon plus 700 for the bread, for a grand total of 7,450, good enough for three days, give or take). Personally, I've made the Fool's Gold Loaf at two Elvis birthday parties I've hosted. They were both good—gooey while hot, and absolutely addictive when cold. But I've never finished one on my own.

V. G. Burgers
3267 28th St., Boulder
303-440-2400
www.vgburgers.com

The first of perhaps a nationwide chain of vegan fast-food joints, V. G. Burgers is pure Boulder, serving up meatless burgers and hot dogs, salads, baked fries, and soy shakes. The packaging and cups are veggie-derived as well and fully compostable, and the grill runs on wind power.

Great Fruitcake Toss
Manitou Springs
www.manitousprings.org

There may be no better way to ring in a new year than putting an unwanted holiday fruitcake to good use by heaving it toward the heavens and hearing it come down with a resound-

ing splat. With different weight classes and events (including mechanical fruitcake launches, human-powered tosses, and spatula-based relays), the Great Fruitcake Tosses have been held in early January since 1995. As of 2007, the record toss eclipsed 300 feet and the best all-time launch was an astounding 1,420 feet.

Green Chile

The spicy stew known as green chile is something of a religion in Denver, and like many Denverites I'm a bit of an extremist. The hotter, the better, just keep my water glass filled and the beers coming. I want to feel the pain; I want to go to the other side. Brow sweating, endorphins rushing, hunkered down over an especially hot bowl or plate, worshipping the fire god by letting him dance on my tongue, I'm in rapture, simultaneously a heavenly and hellish experience, but mostly the former. Denver eateries that are known for their green chile each have their own unique spin on the dish, ranging from vegetarian to pork-centric, from mild to inferno.

The best places to get a bowl or plate include:

Jack-N-Grill
2524 Federal Blvd., Denver, 303-964-9544

Brewery Bar II
150 Kalamath St., Denver, 303-893-0971

El Tejado
2651 S. Broadway Ave., Denver, 303-722-3987

Denver Omelet

Named after the Mile High City, the origin of this three-egg, ham, green pepper, and onion diner staple is somewhat hazy. It seems eggs would often go bad on pioneer expeditions out  West, so onions and spices became popular ingredients in egg dishes in order to mask the deteriorating flavor. Meanwhile, Chinese cooks on railroad crews would approximate egg foo yung with available ingredients (i.e., ham, green pepper, and onions) as French Basques in the Sierra Nevada brought real omelet traditions to the Wild West. In the early 1900s, these traditions intersected and evolved into egg sandwiches and omelets alternately labeled "Western" and "Denver." Today, Denver omelets are available in just about every greasy spoon in the country, but the exact reason for their moniker remains a mystery.

The best places to eat one are:

Davies' Chuck Wagon Diner
9495 W. Colfax Ave., Denver, 303-237-5252

The Breakfast King
1100 S. Santa Fe Dr., Denver, 303-733-0795

Casa Bonita
6715 W. Colfax Ave., Lakewood
303-232-5115
www.casabonitadenver.com

Said to be the largest restaurant in the Western Hemisphere and without doubt one of the tackiest, Casa Bonita opened in the 1970s as a flagship for a chain that stretched from

Little Rock to suburban Denver. The Mile High City's Casa Bonita is 52,000 square feet of sensory overload, centered on a two-story faux cliff with a pool underneath where costumed high-schoolers perform skits, inevitably ending with several if not all of the characters soaking wet. There are also fake caves, a mariachi band, a bizarre monkey mascot, an arcade, and little flags you raise when you want more food, which isn't held in high regard. I sneak salsa and tequila in when I go, which helps a little.

Federal Boulevard

There is no better place in the Rockies to scour for hole-in-the-wall eateries than Federal Boulevard. The long and gritty street bisecting the west side of Denver is loaded with scads of authentic Vietnamese, Mexican, and other ethnic restaurants, not to mention interesting hybrids of several culinary traditions. Reliable picks include:

T-Wa Inn
555 S. Federal Blvd., Denver, 303-922-4584

Jack-N-Grill
2524 Federal Blvd., Denver, 303-964-9544

New Saigon
630 S. Federal Blvd., Denver, 303-936-4954

Tacos y Salsas
910 S. Federal Blvd., Denver, 303-922-9400

SLEEPS

The Curtis Hotel
1405 Curtis St., Denver
330-571-0300
www.thecurtis.com

Reopened in 2007, the Curtis Hotel was remodeled and transformed into an unusual pop-culture-themed lodging, each floor sporting a different theme, such as "Big Hair," "TV Mania," and "Sci Fi." (I'm partial to the "Thirteenth Floor," dedicated to the horror and imagery of *Psycho*'s Bates Motel and Jack Nicholson from *The Shining*.) Other cool touches: wake-up calls from Elvis and Darth Vader soundalikes, a house robot in the lobby, and desk clerks trained in Rock, Paper, Scissors.

Boulder Outlook Hotel and Suites

800 28th St., Boulder
303-443-3322
www.boulderoutlook.com

The most regionally specific place to stay on the Front Range, the Outlook is pure Boulder, from its climbing wall and fenced dog run to its zero-waste policy and killer hot tub. A colorful and inspired reinvention of a former chain property, the Outlook is hard to beat for an affordable, convenient place to bunk down in the People's Republic of Boulder.

HOSTELS

Boulder International Hostel

1107 12th St., Boulder
303-442-0522
www.boulderhostel.com

Denver's Hostel of the Rockies

1717 Race St., Denver
303-861-7777
www.innkeeperrockies.com

The Boulder International Hostel is essentially on CU's campus, with a long history and 400 beds spread over thirteen buildings. Denver's Hostel of the Rockies has a much shorter history (since 2005) and many fewer beds (fifty) in a converted apartment building, private rooms in a different building nearby. Travelers on just about any budget should be able to swing the rent at either place, around $20 a night.

MISC.

Rockmount Ranch Wear
1626 Wazee St., Denver
303-629-7777
www.rockmount.com

Established in LoDo in 1946—long before lower downtown Denver had its clever nickname—Rockmount Ranch Wear is a Colorado original. Founder Jack A. Weil started setting trends long ago, inventing the Western shirt with snaps instead of buttons and making the first commercially produced bolo ties. Their past and present catalogs are full of Western shirts that are wearable works of art, bearing flames, flowers, skulls, guns, cowgirls, poker hands, and just about any other embroidery you can imagine. While Rockmount shirts, hats, and other products are still made in Colorado, their former factory in LoDo is now the company's HQ as well as a great retail store, a museum of Western wear, and a truly can't-miss Denver attraction.

The Beats in Denver

During the summer of 1947, a literary movement sprouted in Denver. Eventually dubbed "The Beat Generation" and associated with Jack Kerouac, Allen Ginsberg, William Burroughs, and other famed wordsmiths, the catalyst for the world-weary, hitchhiking, freight-hopping, free-thinking lifestyle that defined the Beats was Denver's most renowned juvenile delinquent ever, Neal Cassady.

Among Denver's locales frequented by Cassady, mentioned in Kerouac's *On the Road*, or otherwise prominently figuring into Beat history, are the Colburn Hotel (10th Ave. and Grant St.), Sonny Lawson Field (Park Avenue W. and Welton St.), My Brother's Bar (15th St. and Platte St.), Confluence Park (at the intersection of the Platte River and Cherry Creek), and Larimer Street between 20th and 22nd Streets.

Lyons Classic Pinball
339-A Main St., Lyons
303-823-6100
www.lyonspinball.com

As something of a pinball academic—my master's thesis was on the subject of pinball addiction—this is the best place in the Rockies to go for a fix. The arcade houses nearly forty games from the 1950s to today and hosts a pinball tournament the third Thursday of every month. Next door (in the basement of the Oskar Blues brewpub) is Lyons Classic Video, featuring such 1980s gems as *Asteroids, Donkey Kong,* and *Dig Dug.* For my quarters, there is no better way to revisit childhood than playing a game that hooked you when you were twelve years old.

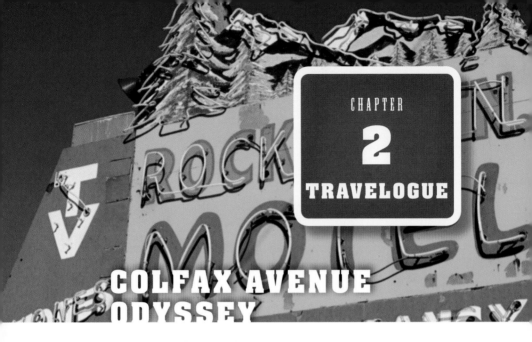

COLFAX AVENUE ODYSSEY

3 DAYS, 30 MILES
(IF YOU COUNT THE BACKTRACKS)

On far East Colfax Avenue, about a dozen miles east of
the Colorado State Capitol and downtown Denver, I spy a
Western clothing store, signified by the fake horse on the
roof. It's as good a place as any to park my car.

I'm nervously preparing to embark on a road trip
unlike any road trip I've ever taken: one road—Colfax
Avenue, the longest urban street in the United States, with
a lusty, druggy, and shady reputation to match—about
twenty-five miles, and no car. I also have no lodging
reservations and no idea what I'm going to do, except walk
the avenue from end to end, east to west, Great Plains to
Rocky Mountain foothills.

I zip in front of another car and make a quick U-turn
before settling into the parking lot of Lancaster's Western
Wear, 18885 East Colfax Avenue, right next door to a bar
and liquor store and in the general vicinity of little else.
Inside, cowboys are shopping for hats and jeans, and an
employee asks if he can help me with anything.

"Hi, um, I'm a travel writer and I'm about to walk down Colfax to the other end," I tell him. "I was wondering if I could park my car here for a couple of days?"

He looks as if I told him I had communicable insanity. After a very long few seconds, he tells me, "You can leave it up in front by the liquor store sign."

"Nobody will mess with it? I won't get ticketed or towed?"

"No, but it does get pretty busy here on the weekends."

"I'll be back before then. I hope."

It's 2 p.m. on a Tuesday. I move my car where advised and start walking west on the sidewalk, which quickly becomes asphalt then dirt then sidewalk again. Light traffic zooms by at fifty-five miles an hour, not a pedestrian in sight, or much of anything else, slightly rural, slightly industrial, just barely suburban.

Soon other automobile-free life-forms make their presence known: There are prairie dogs in burrows dotting the omnipresent vacant lots. They paradoxically shriek while wagging their tails, not too sure about the only pedestrian they may have seen all day out here.

My mind rewinds to minutes before I left my house, when I was packing my laptop, camera, toothbrush, and spare socks and underwear tightly into my backpack. The phone rang; it was my old friend Barnes, working on a movie in New York. He complained about the director's incompetence before I told him of my plans.

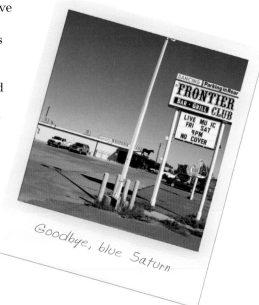

Goodbye, blue Saturn

"Sounds kind of like *Into the Wild*," he commented.

"Except I'm walking in the city, and stopping right when I get to the mountains."

I trudge ahead, taking note of a prairie dog burrow that is essentially part of the sidewalk. After passing vacant lots, trailer parks, warehouses, and what might be the only deer-crossing sign on the entire street, I encounter my first pedestrian a mile or two into the journey, a guy with a shaved head and dark shades.

"What's happening?" I ask.

"What's happening?" comes his mirror reply.

This first interaction calms my nerves a bit. I'm edgier now than when I hike alone in Yellowstone's grizzly bear country. Colfax has the reputation of being both sleazy and dangerous, and not necessarily in that order. Most of its motels seem to cater to prostitutes and crackheads, of which I am neither. To me, this trip is in fact scarier than heading into the wild.

But the scenery quickly changes. I pass a shiny new Ethiopian restaurant before long, its newness and gold-domed grandiosity a surprise to me this far east, and more and more pedestrians cross my path. Fast-food restaurants pop up, as do check-cashing places, liquor stores, and supermarkets. Development gradually overtakes the empty lots. I know I'm really getting somewhere when I spot an

overweight girl at the bus stop, wearing puppy-dog slippers and smoking a Marlboro 100.

Soon enough I'm in the thick of Aurora, Colorado's third-biggest city and the sprawling suburb that flanks Denver to the east. I cross Chambers Avenue and enjoy the shade of the I-225 overpass.

Spanish signs for mercados and other businesses predominate as I wander amongst more pedestrians than I have all afternoon. Most passersby are friendly, but a few don't respond to my "howdies" and "hellos." One of the few Caucasians I see is a fellow with a sideways ballcap and the slogan "Pure Playa" on his shirt. In fact, I see him twice; both times waiting at bus stops I walk past.

The landscape becomes unfamiliar as I pass the massive redevelopment at the former Fitzsimons Army Medical Center, now in the process of becoming a state-of-the-art medical campus. Vibrant flowerbeds and mirrored glass towers provide a marked contrast to the doomed but not yet bulldozed motels and bars across the street, condemned and fenced off.

The next point of interest is Mon Chalet, a swingers' motel that was on my list of possible lodgings. It's only 3 p.m., however, and besides, my girlfriend is probably not too keen on the swinging scene, nor am I now that I really think about it.

A mile later, in Aurora's historic core, an apparently homeless gentleman at a pay phone asks me for the time.

"5:06 p.m.," I tell him.

"Whoo-eee!" he shouts, sounding both confused and jubilant. "Well, at least I got a lot accomplished today."

I, too, feel I have accomplished quite a bit and need a break. The sun is beating down. Unlike most of my backpacking experiences, beer and air-conditioning are readily available on Colfax. I stop in at a bar, the San Marcos Night Club.

"Hola," greets a waitress as I grab a seat at the bar.

"Hi," I respond, squinting at the beers behind the bar.

She switches to English. "What would you like?"

"Um, cerveza...Dos Equis."

She brings me my beer and I greedily drink it down, enjoying the rest but knowing I need to walk about five more miles: eighty blocks down and eighty to go.

The San Marcos is a nice enough spot, a cavernous dance club I imagine really hops on weekend nights. The music and surrounding conversations are all in Spanish. I finish my beer and get two quick queries if I'd like another, but decline and continue west on Colfax.

From the bar, I cross the avenue to inspect the relatively new Martin Luther King Library, just west of the newly restored Fox Theatre. An interpretive display tells the area's history, from the trolley era, that lasted until 1920, then the automobile era when Colfax—a.k.a. U.S. 40—was an unavoidable thoroughfare from the East Coast to the West. But a steep decline followed once the interstate era commenced in the 1950s.

A chair for a big blue bear?

Thankfully, the strip saw an "abrupt" turnaround in the 1990s, thanks to all sorts of projects nearby, the display concluded. It looks more like a work in progress to me, but it feels authentically American even if it is one. On the next corner west, a guy in a green bandana is taking a photo of an oversized blue chair screwed into the sidewalk. I start talking to him, turns out he's the sculptor Chris Weed. I introduce myself and tell him what I'm doing.

"Watch out," he warns.

Westbound, I pass moldy motels, plenty of fast-food and payday-loan joints, liquor stores, and tattoo parlors. I also see a barber shop with a huge poster of Louis Farrakhan, a hip-hop recording studio, Little Baba's Market, the all-nude Saturdays

strip club, and finally a Starbucks—the first I've seen in walking seven miles west on Colfax. But as the sun sets behind downtown Denver, the pedestrian traffic drops off precipitously, not unlike at my rural eastern starting point.

I take a mental inventory of all of the different trash I've seen strewn on the sidewalk. Cigarette butts, glass, dog shit, a rusted mailbox, the mesh linings of swim trunks without the trunks, condoms, an armchair, an application for a job at Bimbo Bakery that never saw a pencil.

My feet, legs, lungs, eyes, and pretty much everything else are getting fatigued. I press on, determined to make it into a hipper area to hang my hat for the night. And soon enough, I'm seeing signs of gentrification mixed in with the urban squalor: wine and espresso bars, doggie daycare, hip furniture stores, and yoga. I cross bustling Colorado Boulevard and the nearby street my girlfriend Ruthie lives on, just a few short blocks from Colfax.

But I continue west, never diverting from Colfax, stopping a couple of blocks later for a beer at a neighborhood watering hole, the P. S. Lounge. I take a seat at the bar under an over-sized visage of Elvis and drink four glasses of water with my beer and complimentary shot. It would be easy for me to be an alcoholic if I wandered this street without a car or a home. After a little small talk with a fellow patron, I'm off, aiming for the All-Inn, a full 9.9 miles from Lancaster's Western Wear and a world away, tucked amidst the movie palace turned porn palace turned music venue the Bluebird Theater, hip bars, hip shops, and hip new apartment buildings.

I warily walk into the lobby, which is surprisingly clean, wait my turn after a Mexican father and son, and ask to see a room. The clerk asks to hold my ID—never a good sign—and tells me there is a $5 key deposit—another bad sign. But I persist and am mildly surprised by the mediocre room. At least it's not awful, well, not too awful. I've had worse—just barely. I give the clerk $56, she gives me my ID back and the remote control to the TV in my room.

I take a load off and call Ruthie, who agrees to meet me for a drink at nearby Mezcal. I beat her to a barstool and

order a PBR. Ruthie shows up and I preface a hug-and-kiss hello with "I probably smell like sweat and exhaust."

We hug and she surprises me with "You smell good."

"Maybe sweat and exhaust mix nicely."

"Maybe sweat and exhaust are an aphrodisiac," she says seductively.

I soon am hungrily gobbling down some of the best huevos rancheros I've had in my life. I ask Ruthie if she'd like to see my room at the All-Inn.

Unfortunately, the scent of intermingling exhaust and sweat are apparently canceled out by the visual and aromatic stimuli of a room at the All-Inn. Ruthie is somewhat aghast by the room's warts and smiles broadly when an ambulance screams by on Colfax.

Drunk food extraordinaire

I walk Ruthie home but refuse her pull off of Colfax when we hit her north-south street. "No," I tell her. "Must stay on Colfax."

Soon after kissing her goodnight, I'm on a barstool at the Lion's Lair, just a half-mile west of the All-Inn. The quasi-legendary punk-rock dive is hosting an open mic, and I'm sitting next to a graying, bearded guy named Dave who spends his winters in Antarctica at McMurdo Station.

Shooting the shit, I ask Dave about how Antarctica compares to Colfax.

"I've run into a couple of people here on Colfax I knew down there," he answers. Small world. I prod and he tells me about the bars and coffee shops at McMurdo, the movie theaters and the gift shop.

The crowd at the Lair is diverse, ranging from Caucasians in their twenties to African-Americans in their

fifties. I watch the Rockies take a lead into the ninth inning and slap five with a guy with cornrows before splitting into the dark night.

I watch the Rockies win in my room before hitting up the All-Inn's resident RockBar for a nightcap. Somehow cheesy and chic, the place is like a 1970s bug in amber: The bar was renovated in 1977 but never used, sealed for nearly thirty years until new ownership reopened it in 2006. John Denver used to play here, I've been told. The manager, Robert, tells me they cleaned it up, but nearly everything, from the patterned carpeting to the mirrored walls, is original, even the odd cache of porn clippings hidden behind a cabinet above the bar.

Robert takes leave, but his girlfriend remains. She asks if I walk on Colfax, says I look familiar. I tell her no, not usually, but I've walked ten miles on it today. She probably saw me as I passed her apartment earlier, we concur. I tell her that I was surprised by how many people I saw twice, thinking not only of "Pure Playa" but also a guy with a cane, a professional-looking woman, the bartender at the San Marcos, and a panhandler.

At the stroke of midnight, buzzed, I slip up the staircase to room 213. At the end of the day, worming my way deeper and deeper into humanity's hive on Colfax was comparably scary to hiking in bear country, which is to say not very scary at all.

Beams of red neon filtered by broken parallel shades, traffic noise, and the smell of stale cigarettes make for a night of fitful sleep, and rush hour turns the traffic volume all the way up around 7 a.m. With the new day comes sunlight to

The infamous Lair

illuminate the room's quirks. Burns and stains on the carpet, more scratches and grime than I'd initially noticed, and all sorts of maintenance issues, large and small. I take a quick shower and check out. The clerk gives me my $5 deposit back when I turn in my key.

After a coffee, I resume my easterly rambling, a crisp fall breeze in the air. I pass another Starbucks and then see many trappings of revitalization I missed the night before. One storefront features a poster of an unruly kid in his Sunday best, with the slogan "Colfax Cleans Up Pretty Good." There is also still plenty of sleaze, most visibly in the form of adult bookstores with jerk-off video booths in the back. Then I get my biggest scare of the trip thus far when an ornery little dachshund barks at me from his front porch.

I divert into Denver's beloved Tattered Cover bookstore, which traded its longtime location in chichi Cherry Creek for Colfax in 2006 and is now the shining star of East Colfax, rising the anchor of a major re-development of a long-vacant theater. I don't buy a book before leaving because my pack is too full and I haven't read one page of the book I do have.

Slightly hungover, I meander into Pete's Kitchen, a venerable diner slinging hash since 1942. Strangely enough, there is no Denver omelet on the menu, so I opt for two eggs over easy, hash browns, and toast. My order is up in literally two minutes, and soon I am scraping up the last of the runny yolk with the last of the hash browns.

Cobwebs cleared, 10:30 a.m., I'm once again wandering west, passing a ragged woman in hot pink thigh-high boots at a bus stop. People are more numerous on this stretch of Colfax, there are more adult emporiums with the

Charlie reading forevermore

jerk-off booths in the back (busy even at this hour), and the extreme fringe is much crazier. I see the trip's first drunk passed out on the sidewalk right in front of the Colorado State Capitol, nearly twelve miles from where I started a day before.

The latest official marker

Soon I'm on the Capitol steps, taking photos of four Dutch tourists at the engraving on the fifteenth step marking the 1947 estimate for a mile above sea level, which was since moved up two steps then down five steps when modern technology provided a more accurate reading. "Say gouda!"

They take my picture ("Say whiskey!"), we exchange pleasantries about Amsterdam and Denver, and we go our separate ways. I go inside for a tour. Up on top of the dome, Celina tells me that its unmistakable plating is made up of a mere three pounds of 24-karat gold, replaced once every thirty years. The old gold is simply scraped off into the wind.

Celina also tells me the crack in the central staircase is from a man who jumped from the third level, killing himself "because I can't have my Baby Doe," as he put it in his suicide note, inexplicably, because he knew no Baby Doe.

In the museum below, I snap a shot of something else inexplicable: a replica of the Capitol made of canned goods, including anchovies, spaghetti sauce, condensed milk, and a single bottle of water crowning the sardine-can dome. On my way out, a quote on the wall describes the building as "The heart of Colorado."

Soon I'm being shown around the main level by a gracious and cheerful volunteer named Ed, an older gentleman whose grandfather worked as a stonemason when they built the Capitol. He tips me off to some of the interesting details in the stonework, lays on his back to help a tourist get a worm's-eye photo of the underside of the dome, and illuminates a series of historic murals.

I tell Ed of my east-to-west quest and he cracks a smile. "Oh, I can show you where all of the whorehouses are," he quips, grabbing a map. But he tells me to check out something much different: the stained glass windows in the nearby Cathedral Basilica of the Immaculate Conception. (He also tells me how East Colfax is historically the domain of progressive Jews and West Colfax that of Orthodox Jews.) I heed his advice and backtrack three blocks after exiting the Capitol.

The sanctity of the scene inside the church is jarring, especially in contrast to the chaos outside, the surrounding video peep shows, tattoo parlors, and bars attracting society's undercrust. People are quietly praying in this work of beautiful art. I've walked and driven by this place hundreds of times, but never before actually seen the window made of 30,000 pieces of stained glass, until now.

I take my Communion in the form of a veal schnitzel sandwich in nearby Civic Center Park, best known for its shady reputation and drug trade but today hosting an "outdoor market and café," complete with bluegrass entertainment.

Here, on the southern tip of downtown Denver, the city's diversity hits a crescendo, with people of every race and class and description—tourists, panhandlers, lawyers, professionals, bike messengers, drug fiends, students, politicians, secretaries.

People-watching, resting my blistered feet, and polishing off the schnitzel, I think I could sit on this shady patch of grass for a couple of hours. My walk only halfway complete, however, the clock is ticking if I want to make it to Casa Bonita for dinner.

The pedestrian traffic thins markedly as I march up the bridge over the railroad tracks, the Platte River, and I-25. A little ways behind me is one lone guy in a red vest I've seen on and off since I was downtown. He catches up when I stop

to take some photos. I quickly notice his black eye and the drool on his lip and beard. He shows me a piece of paper with an address, some sort of medical release.

"You're getting there," I tell him. "Maybe another mile."

"Do you have a cigarette?" he growls.

When I tell him I don't, he glares at me angrily. I hope this encounter isn't a bad omen. The next two omens are better, a kid on a blinged-and-chromed-out bike going the opposite way and a seventy-year-old on a bike who passed me and said he'd complain but nobody would listen, then went on to complain anyway.

After cresting a hill, the bridge ends before the Federal Boulevard overpass, with the home of the Denver Broncos in view—unfortunately named Invesco Field at Mile High. I see a route down to the stadium, which is on Colfax for all practical purposes, and decide to see what I could see.

For the first time, I realize just how anatomically correct some of the bronco sculptures are. In the store, I also find out that famed Broncomaniac the Barrel Man has his own bobblehead doll. I consider an orange-and-blue throwback leather helmet, but walk out only with a post-card and a refilled water bottle.

While I've technically been on West Colfax since lunch, I am soon being greeted by a heavily tagged "West Colfax Welcomes You" sign. Behind it, kids play soccer in a school-yard, but the liquor stores and tattoo parlors dominate the avenue in just a few blocks. I pass a porno theater (with an elderly gentleman entering) and the steam baths, and decide—like the day before at Mon Chalet—to take a rain check.

But I need a break. I'm getting tired, my film camera is out of batteries, and my digital camera is full. I decide to stop at a gnarly little dive called the Viking for a cold draft beer and an opportunity to empty my digital photos onto my laptop.

"There's no Wi-Fi here," advises a guy with a Michigan cap.

"I know. I'm just out of memory on my digital camera."

We start talking. I tell him of my journey on Colfax.

"It's an interesting street," he says. "It changes so much."

"I'm not showing you room! No way!"

He's a middle-aged black guy and former G.I. and current bus driver on Colfax. He tells me of living in Sweden and visiting Morocco, describing the latter as a multicultural crossroads, European, Asian, African, and Middle Eastern.

"Kind of like Colfax," I crack.

"Yep," he laughs, then heads to the bar to chat up a female.

My mug and digital camera both empty, I resume my west-ward course, leaving Denver and entering Lakewood, my feet aching worse and worse by the block. I need rest. And my dinner destination—the world famous, locally infamous Casa Bonita—is right across the street.

Spying the Big Bunny Motel, formerly the Bugs Bunny until Warner Bros. lawyers got involved, I decide to see if I can look at a room. The office is locked, so I ring a doorbell, summoning a stern-looking Asian woman. She lets me inside and slips behind the front desk, shielded by bulletproof glass. A notice about a police crackdown on methamphetamine labs hangs prominently on the wall.

"How much for a room?" I ask.

"Thirty dollar."

"Can you show me one of them?"

For some reason, these were the magic words to make the woman go ballistic.

"No!" she yells. "Thirty dollar is cheap—I'm not showing you room! No way!" She leaves me alone at the desk, retreating into her living quarters as she curses me in at least two languages.

Dumbfounded, I stand there, wondering if a more reasonable person might come and try and do business with me. No such luck. I leave, perturbed and tired, hoping a decent motel appears on the horizon soon.

Somehow one does. While certainly a one-star affair, the Denver West Inn is above the zero-star norm on Colfax, with stained carpet but overall much better accommodations than the All-Inn. Once inside my $50 room, I strip out of my sweaty shirt and socks and mull over the day for a little while before calling Ruthie to arrange for our dinner at Casa Bonita.

An hour and a shower later, we're in the labyrinthine cafeteria-style line, which sometimes snakes around for more than an hour on weekends, but only twenty minutes this Wednesday. I ask Ruthie how much gold she thinks is on the Capitol dome.

She guesses 100,000 pounds. I break the bad news that it's only three.

"Three pounds—are you kidding me?" she asks incredulously.

"100,000 pounds—are you kidding *me*?" I reply.

Ruthie's a devout vegetarian, so we both get the only meatless option: cheese enchiladas with beans and rice. It's the cheese that scares me, bright yellow glop that in no way appears to be part of the dairy food group.

She swears she really didn't lick the skull

But as my stomach and muscles and glands all demand protein and sugar and salt, it's surprisingly edible, and the salsa is better than it is in my memory. I can't tell if the place has improved or if my body's need for sustenance has skewed my taste buds, but it's not half bad.

It's Ruthie's first time at Casa Bonita (I've been going since childhood), so I give her the grand tour: spooky Black Bart's Cave, the faux cliffs in the center that teenage employees dive from for the entertainment of the diners, and the video arcade. Her review: "This place is ridiculous."

At the gift shop, I describe the pink monkey mascot that once frequented the place, scaring the children, and locate a pack of souvenir stickers that prominently feature said pink monkey. Paying the cashier for the stickers, I inquire about the fuchsia primate. He knows nothing of it, and he's been working here for nearly five months.

They need to bring that monkey back.

Ruthie gives me a ride back to my motel and keeps me company for an hour or so. After she leaves, oh so tired, the Rockies win their tenth game in a row, and, oh so tired, I fall soundly asleep.

I wake a full eight hours later to someone having an animated phone conversation in the next room. The walls are just thin enough to let sound in, but thick enough to render it indecipherable.

Mmmmm... Denver omelet good

Groggy, I pull the phone book out of the nightstand and turn on the light. Davies' Chuck Wagon Diner, my breakfast destination, is twenty-three blocks west. Heritage Square, the amusement park near the end of the road, is 110 blocks west, around twenty-five miles from where I parked my car.

The bed is hard to give up, but hunger and coffee addiction prevail. (My room has a coffeemaker with a label taped on it: "We provide the coffeemaker and warmer, you bring your own coffee.")

After a shower, I'm back on my way west by 8:45 a.m. From the

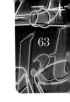

outset, the sidewalks are pretty desolate, only the rare pass-erby on foot. I see my first Wal-Mart on Colfax here, about sixteen miles into my walk. Cars again dominate; one guy trying to turn as I'm in the crosswalk gestures madly for me to speed up for his impatient ass. I keep my slow pace and glare at him through my sunglasses. I hope I don't seem like such an asshole when I'm behind the wheel.

Then I see the big cowboy marking the spot of Davies' Chuck Wagon Diner, an authentic prefabricated diner made in New Jersey, delivered here by rail, and perhaps the country's westernmost one in operation. On top is a big plastic horse, not unlike the one at Lancaster's at the begin-ning of the line.

There is a Denver omelet on the menu, so I order it with cheddar cheese and a side of pancakes. I need fuel for the mostly uphill trek in front of me. Soon I'm slathering my last hunks of hash browns and omelet with the house habañero sauce, washing it down with black coffee. I buy a postcard as I pay my check.

Then I'm cresting Golden Hill, the mountains looming ever closer, just a few miles away. The views get better and better, and development melts away, as do the sidewalks. A sign at one vacant lot promises luxury condos are in the works.

Atop the hill, weeds nearly obscure an Orthodox Jewish graveyard, its resident headstones inscribed in Hebrew, most death dates in the 1930s. There is no fence on the western boundary, so I wander in and take a few photos. The thorny greenery taking over the peaceful scene reminds me that it's not the destination that's truly important, but the journey.

Just a little farther is the first rest stop I've seen on more than twenty miles of Colfax Avenue, a place that must have served plenty of cross-country motorists when U.S. 40 was the only option. But nobody is here today. Signs commemorate the road as the Blue Star Memorial Highway, a tribute to American veterans of foreign wars; two shaded picnic tables with grills overlook the nicely treed neighborhood below.

A picnic table beckons; I take off my pack and drink some water. The roar of passing cars fades as I think about my mood on the walk, which has ranged from pure bliss to anxiousness to get home and be done with the trip. Does it matter one iota when I do actually get home? I'll almost certainly still get home sometime, and the journey won't end even when I arrive.

There is no sidewalk on the downslope of Golden Hill, and the westbound emergency lane disappears into over-growth. Fearing the journey might actually end right here with me getting run over, I dodge across to the south side of the street and find a well-worn trail through the roadside thicket. Soon the cement sidewalk reappears as the earth tilts back up, the first big swell of the Rockies. The open space is consumed by impersonal post-suburban develop-ment, a huge outdoor maze of big boxes, car dealerships, and office parks.

In front of me is the first curve I've encountered on my twenty-plus miles on Colfax thus far, slicing southwest as it parallels the main artery for traffic, I-70, which it merges with in just a mile or so. As I plod ever so close to the Rockies, I feel great. I have no desire to get home, or for that matter any other place in particular, any faster than I should get there.

The sidewalk becomes a trail through the thorny roadside flora again. The grade increases. I'm in the foothills, the mountains are right there. Storage units and biker bars and craggy rock formations dot the roadside. After a last beer and a glass of water at Susie's Bar and Grill, I see the second deer cross-ing sign on Colfax.

Resting in peace on West Colfax

Traipsing into the nearly forgotten amusement park Heritage Square, I push westward, past the open gift shops and closed rides, toward the mountains. Behind the miniature railroad I spy a trail: the Apex Trail, a sign informs me, once the main route west, the pre-petroleum predecessor to the highways. I ignore my blistered feet and continue up the trail.

I meet a hiker coming down. We chat and I tell him where I started. "That's a long trip," he says. I'm hoping he will assure me this is as good a spot as any to end my trek, but he says, "Colfax keeps going for quite a ways, in a sense," referring to U.S. 40, which once connected Atlantic City and San Francisco.

He's right, of course, but it's time for me to stop. I scurry up to an incredible overlook and enjoy the view with several long drinks of water, Colfax Avenue arcing north and bee-lining east, between the spires of downtown and the gold speck of the Capitol dome, before knifing into the plains farther than my eyes can see.

Where to go...

Lancaster's Western Wear
18885 E. Colfax Ave., Aurora
303-343-0318

Mon Chalet
12033 E. Colfax Ave., Aurora
303-364-2643
www.mon-chalet.com

San Marcos Night Club
9935 E. Colfax Ave., Aurora
303-341-2939

P. S. Lounge
3416 E. Colfax Ave., Denver
303-320-1200

All-Inn
3015 E. Colfax Ave., Denver
303-388-4811

Mezcal
3230 E. Colfax Ave., Denver
303-322-5219

Lion's Lair
2022 E. Colfax Ave., Denver
303-320-9200
www.nipp.com

RockBar
3015 E. Colfax Ave., Denver
303-322-4444

Tattered Cover
2526 E. Colfax Ave., Denver
303-322-7727
www.tatteredcover.com

Pete's Kitchen
1962 E. Colfax Ave., Denver
303-321-3139

Colorado State Capitol
200 E. Colfax Ave., Denver
303-866-2604

Cathedral Basilica of the Immaculate Conception
400 E. Colfax Ave., Denver
303-831-7010
www.archden.org

Invesco Field at Mile High
W. Colfax Ave. at I-25, Denver
720-258-3000
www.invescofield.com

Viking
4888 W. Colfax Ave., Denver
303-623-3256

Denver West Inn
7150 W. Colfax Ave., Lakewood
303-238-1251

Casa Bonita
6715 W. Colfax Ave., Lakewood
303-232-5115
www.casabonitadenver.com

Davies' Chuck Wagon Diner
9495 W. Colfax Ave., Lakewood
303-237-5252

Susie's Bar and Grill
17999 W. Colfax Ave., Golden
303-278-9000

Heritage Square
18301 W. Colfax Ave., Golden
303-279-2789
www.heritagesquare.info

THE NAPA VALLEY OF BEER

4 DAYS, 260 MILES

Just before noon at Oskar Blues Brewery in laid-back Lyons, I have my first drink of beer, a two-ounce sample of Oskar Blues Brewery's Gordon. The hoppy ale passes the gateway of my mouth, leaving a tingling partial numbness in its wake, en route to my stomach, where a nice warm sensation satiates my preexisting hunger. Next up, the bloodstream, then the brain, and before long the bladder, as the transformation subtly begins.

I can't resist the brewpub's vintage arcade: *Frogger*, *Asteroids*, and *Elevator Action* all beep and beckon. Change for a dollar. One quarter goes to Paperboy. Two dismal minutes later, I plunk another into Gorf. Then on Q*Bert I finally show a hint of talent, hopping to the second level.

After entering "EMP" for posterity, I wander outside to see if the bus has arrived yet. As a preamble to Denver's annual Great American Beer Festival (GABF), a Boulder County Brews Cruise is hauling visiting beer nuts to three area breweries and one area meadery. Near a ten-foot tower of yet-to-be-filled Old Chub cans, I see Dale Katechis and Marty Jones, the brewery's founder and "lead singer," respectively.

"I think I lost all of my video game skills," I tell them. "It might be the years of drinking."

"I always seem to play better when I have at least one beer in me," Marty advises.

I'd hitched a ride from Denver to Lyons with Marty, a Virginia-born beer writer, beer publicist, songwriter of beer-soaked songs, and also one of the nicest guys involved in Colorado's remarkable beer culture.

In fact, Marty moved to Denver because of the wealth of great breweries and taprooms we have in the Front Range—Colorado brews more beer per capita than even Wisconsin, with ninety-two breweries statewide. Marty even honeymooned with his wife, Lisa—who I'd met at his place earlier, along with their French bulldogs, Guernsey and Barley—at the 1991 GABF. What a concept for a honeymoon.

The October spectacular is the beer world's Oscars and World Series rolled into one, with three nights of open sessions surrounding an awards ceremony. Open sessions each attract more than 10,000 patrons to sample the wares of breweries from all over the country: This year, it's 408 breweries and 1,884 beers. If you manage to quaff one-ounce samples of them all, you will have consumed 157 beers in four days, a truly Herculean feat. (I doubt it's ever been done, but then again I don't know if the late legendary wrestler/actor/drinker Andre the Giant ever attended.)

A very big vat

Allow me to reiterate: a festival of more than 10,000 people trying to see how many beers they can sample in four-and-a-half hours. And it kicks off tomorrow night.

On the drive up, Marty and I talk about Loretta Lynn's voice, still sexy and strong at seventy, and the phenomenon of "fake craft beer" produced by the big-three American breweries. He also cracks me up telling me about the "Fountain of Truth," an invention of Dale's comprised of a keg of beer connected to a drinking fountain.

Sadly, the Fountain of Truth fails to make an appearance during the Brews Cruise stop at the brewery. But as we park, Marty does immediately recognize the inventor of an award-winning coconut porter wandering into Oskar Blues with his friends, all in town for the GABF from Japan, and quickly runs over to shake his hand.

Soon the tour group arrives, a friendly bunch of beer lovers. Before and after the tour of the brewery and adjacent cannery—Oskar Blues is known for the industry's first canned microbrews—I talk to a retired widower named Frank from Oregon and a cheerful woman named Michelle, who tells me a good first line for a novel she may or may not write: "She carried her purse like a six-pack."

Later, I tell Dale I only have a media pass to the Friday open session, and he hooks me up with two spare tickets for Thursday's. I also discuss volunteering to pour beers for Oskar Blues for Saturday's session, which would give me the hat trick: entry into all three open sessions.

Before leaving for Denver—with a little over just one beer in me—I test Marty's theory and give Q*Bert one more shot. He's right: I make it all the way to the third level and the top of the high-score list.

Riding home, it's a sunny October day. Marty and I talk about fishing and music and, of course, beer. His band, Marty Jones and the Brewbadours, is playing at the Falling Rock Tap House downtown later that night. I shake his hand and tell him I'll see him there.

· · · · ·

For three hours I work and coordinate beer fest details with bandmates Duff and Ingvald (we play in an experimental / electronic / psychedelic / heavy metal trio called Weird Al Qaida). At 6 p.m., I take the light rail downtown to meet Ruthie and her roommate Gia at Falling Rock.

It's packed with predominately white male beer geeks. But the ambiance and music are good, the beer is excellent—including a $6 somewhat whiskey-scented West Flemish Urthel beer from a forty-five-liter batch made especially for tonight. (I like it, Ruthie calls it "disgusting," and Gia dubs it "sherry-like" between hiccups.)

After discussing hiccup cures and little-known superheroes such as Cheesemaster and Orange Lantern, I walk Ruthie and Gia to a bus stop, then hoof it back to the Falling Rock for the end of the set by craft-beer industry supergroup Rolling Boil. All is well with the world...

The Rockies are going to the World Series! Let's drink more beer!

Then anger percolates into my jubilance when an unshaven, ballcapped, somewhat aggro bartender for some reason ignores me, going so far as to tell me, "Hey—guess what? It's not your turn next!" while serving people who were clearly behind me. I bite my tongue and keep in mind that some people are hereditary assholes. Then again, maybe it's me. Beer catalyzes rage just as effectively as it froths up happiness, the Dionysian duality of drunkenness, the jester and the madman.

After a few minutes, a mellower barman finally treats me with a modicum of respect and pours me a pint of Oskar Blues' Duke of Lyons from a keg saved from the year before. It's a Belgian sour brown, a very interesting, very sour pint of beer meant to be savored. So I sip it and listen to Marty's second set, which includes a cover of "You Shook Me All Night Long," as well as originals like "Match Made in Milwaukee" and "Someone Take the Bottle from My Hand." At one point his brother Chris jumps on stage and sings his own "Fill My Feeding Tube with Beer."

Cruisers rule!

But my energy is nearly expended, and the music and my beer-buzz my only friends. Ruthie and Gia gone, post-rebuke from the bartender, I am in a crowded room, drinking alone. If I could chug the Duke I would, but it's the polar opposite of a chugging beer. I don't finish it until the end of the show.

It's worth it. But as the Duke starts mingling with his less aristocratic peers in my belly, blood, and brain, my mental carriage becomes a pumpkin. I shake Marty's hand adieu for the second time in nine hours and head for the light rail to make my way home. I stumble in at 1 or so a.m. and try but fail to drink the odd can of corporate beer hanging around in my fridge.

· · · · ·

Thursday. It's beer fest opening day. I have a ticket, Ingvald has a ticket, and Duff has been combing Craigslist all morning. I'm a bit hungover and work until mid-morning before pulling it together for a trip north to Fort Collins.

First I visit the stellar tasting room at the state's largest microbrewery, New Belgium, and take one of the few bar stools available, next to a dude with long blond locks and plenty of facial hair. The place is festive and busy with GABF ticketholders. A bartender gives us a menu and a form to check off which four three-ounce samples we'd like to taste. He also asks us to write down the name of a movie that was a waste of time and money, in an oval below the beers. I check the boxes next to the Trippel, Lips of Faith, Blue Paddle, and 2° Below and write, "*Star Wars*—the one with Jar Jar Binks" in the oval.

"I don't remember," the dude sitting next to me writes in his oval. "I was probably stoned."

We get our beers and start talking—he works in the kitchen at a mountain resort of some kind and is thinking about opening a hostel in Fort Collins. The dude turns out to be a really nice guy and we have a great conversation. Hunter S. Thompson was right: "Good people drink good beer."

I am running out of time and don't want my blood-alcohol content to exceed the legal limit, so I skip a planned stop at one of my favorites, Odell Brewing Company, just a few blocks from New Belgium, and speed south to Left Hand Brewing in Longmont.

A Nebraskan asks a tough-looking guy with a shaved head at the bar if he is in town for the beer fest.

"No, I live here," he responds. "I literally live *here*."

I'm surprised to find out he is a local minister, E. C. (short for Eugene Constantine). "I write my sermons here," he tells me, then declines the offer of another pint from the barkeep. "I have to work the chains at my son's football game—I don't want to be leaning on the first-down marker."

I take a tour of the brewery with about ten other people, but the clock is ticking: Ingvald might be at my house already and Duff has no ticket. I make it home just before 5 p.m., and we take the light rail downtown to the convention center. Duff buys a ticket from a scalper for $90—twice face value—just after we hear a collective roar from the crowd and the gates finally open.

Pour me another!

"Do you think you can drink $90 worth of beer?" I ask him while we wait in the serpentine line.

"I think I can," he replies. "I'm going to try."

At 6 p.m., we're on the festival floor. It's organized by region, featuring breweries from forty-five states and the District of Columbia. (Get with it, Alaska, Alabama, North Dakota, Rhode Island, and West Virginia!) Diving right into the thousands of people milling about from table to table, we start in the Southwest.

At 6:15, I try an interesting black cherry stout from a brewery in Vegas. Soon we work our way to the tables of California, Washington, and Oregon.

At 6:25, I make my official appraisal of the scene: "This place is awesome."

"You're already slurring your words," Ingvald informs me.

One festival volunteer with a goatee and a Crested Butte hat is already hooting and hollering at the top of his lungs for no particular reason. Some girl accuses Ingvald of groping her boob with his elbow as we work our way through the crowd. I try to take notes but usually forget what I want to write by the time I balance my cup, pad, and pen.

Ingvald drops his plastic sampling cup. I start yelling at the top of my lungs, as is GABF tradition, and many others nearby follow my lead. Soon the roar of the crowd envelops all other sounds as Ingvald meekly retrieves his cup from the concrete floor. At least it is intact.

I get separated from Duff and Ingvald at 7:30. I vainly comb the 10,000-person crowd for a half hour, getting angry that I am alone until I see a drunk yelling, "Luke, I am your father" into an industrial-strength fan. I borrow a girl's cell phone—I don't own one—and drool all over it as I call Ingvald. After a breakup that lasted thirty minutes, the band is reunited.

But this is just the first of many separations we have over the next few hours. Ingvald is next to go solo, struggling with a nasty case of the hiccups, as Duff and I agree that Oskar Blues' Gordon might be the cream of the beer-fest crop.

At 9 p.m., we're together again, trying a habañero beer named Ring of Fire. I like it very much. I know I'm irrevocably smashed when I opt for an ounce of Mickey's malt liquor.

At 10 p.m., beer buzzes spill out into the streets of downtown Denver.

Kosta hard at work.

We walk over to Old Curtis Street, one of our favorite downtown hangouts, where we've taken the stage several times in several different bands, and of course we order more beers. Duff and I also order chili rellenos.

But before the food even arrives, Duff mysteriously disappears. Ingvald and I try to locate him but have no luck. We stumble to Bar Bar down the street, one of the diviest dives in town, but he's not there either. Ingvald gets a phone call from an old girlfriend and goes outside to take it.

I finish my beer at the bar alone and go outside. Now I can't find Duff or Ingvald. And I'm very drunk. I wander back to Old Curtis Street and ask proprietor Kosta if he's seen either of them.

"No, man," he says. "You guys want to do another show here sometime?"

Happy to score a Weird Al Qaida gig but otherwise confused and alone, I tell Kosta I'll call soon, then go catch the train south toward my house. The ride is a hazy experience, my short-term memory flickering on and off amidst the perhaps one hundred different kinds of beer coursing through my system.

Once home, I call Ingvald, who is heading south on foot.

"Duff's in jail," he says. "I just talked to him—he said he was in a paddy wagon."

I tell Ingvald to meet me at 3 Kings and get on my bike and start drunk-riding north. (Author's note: I do not condone riding your bike after beer fest. It is never a good idea.) My chain falls off and my hands get covered in black grease as I put it back on, cursing.

After what seems like hours, I make it to the bar and find Ingvald with a whiskey. We again talk to Duff, who rants about where they're taking them, but feel we have no option other than drunk-dialing people who might be able to drive. No luck.

Okay, maybe just top 'er off

One of the 3 Kings' owners, Jim, is behind the bar and on the wagon. His sober advice: Call it a night.

So we try to ride tandem on my bike, but it's a disaster. Ingvald tries to ride it alone, the chain falls off, and he skins his shoulder and chin and scratches his glasses when he crashes. I push the bike the rest of the way home—about three miles—and we split a can of Ten-Fidy before crashing at 4 a.m.

Ingvald wakes me up not quite six hours later, letting me know Duff is taking the bus to my house. I feel like absolute hell, thirsty for water with a bruised brain.

Around 11 a.m., Duff arrives, and not only is he hungover like me but his eye and lip are swollen from a punch in the face that the arresting officer dealt him after the handcuffs went on.

Duff tells us the whole story: "I never black out, but I did last night," he starts. After leaving Old Curtis Street before his rellenos arrived, it seems Duff got on a bus that took him to a strange part of town. The overly aggressive arresting officer then picked him up as he waited for another bus, cuffed him, threw him in the back of his car, punched him, and called the paddy wagon to take him to detox. His blood alcohol was 0.18 percent. Among the memory fragments left in his mind: arguing with someone on the bus, meeting another GABF refugee at the drunk tank, and asking the night clerk where the hell he was.

Press luncheon glassware orgy

"I had a good time at the beer fest," he says.

Duff didn't do anything wrong— no charges were filed. All he did was somewhat intentionally transform from a sober, thoughtful, polite individual into a cackling lunatic with unusually poor judgment, as did thousands of others last night. Ingvald mentions he thought it would have been more like him to land in the drunk tank. I agree.

I have an all-access media pass for Friday night's session. Ingvald and Duff express zero interest in buying a ticket from a scalper. Personally, I don't have any business going either. I consumed more beer in one long evening than I had in a very long time, walked ten miles or so, and slept all of five hours. Everything hurts. I don't even have any business going to the beer-pairing media luncheon I attend at noon.

The iced water and tea do me good, and the food and beer is uniformly terrific. After a salad and New Belgium Mothership Wit, we have beef brisket with Old School Irish Stout from Mountain Sun in Boulder, then a palate cleanser of unusual lemon-basil sorbet with a shot of Oskar Blues' flagship Dale's Pale Ale before brownies with Great Divide Oak Aged Yeti Imperial Stout.

My taste buds, which had pretty much been tossed aside in the first fifteen minutes of the Thursday night session, were telling me that, yes, there was much more to drinking beer than getting drunk.

I make it home at 3 p.m. and enjoy a couple of hours of peace and quiet before returning to the light rail stop and taking a train back to the convention center for round two.

Tonight, I've decided, I'm going for quality over quantity. I have a media pass instead of a paid ticket, so I plan on assuming the role of fly-on-the-wall reporter rather than a werewolf high on moonlight and a gallon of beer.

So I take it much slower on the samples and spend more time taking notes and pictures. I try the new "You Be the

Duff and Ingvald

Judge" exhibit and sit down with a judge to learn what goes into the critiquing for the medals, which will be awarded on Saturday afternoon. I arrange to volunteer Saturday night at the merchandise booth to get a different perspective, as the beer fest relies on an army of nearly 3,000 volunteers.

I see Pete Coors, a guy in monk's robes and ski goggles, people in hop and bottle costumes, Charlie Papazian, and a S.W.A.T. team. I take note of the designated driver area, where five women sip soda pop and gossip next to two drunks taking a load off. I also take note of the best T-shirt slogans I see over the course of the evening: "Beer Me, I'm Irish," "What Would Jesus Brew?" "Jesus Hates Me," "Finish Your Beer: There Are Sober Kids in India," and "I'm Funnier Drunk."

A sign on the wall reads "Savor the Flavor Responsibly." A guys passes by, talking into his cell phone, "Everybody's pretty much wasted."

For me, the beer is not going down nearly as smoothly as it did the night before. I am much pickier, focusing on interesting names (Butthead, Furious IPA, Deranger) and renowned breweries (Odell, Maui Brewing Company, Flying Dog).

My legs and brain jelly, I slump into a lone chair in the corner and take a five-minute break. Now it's time to buck up, I convince myself. Forty-five minutes until last call.

After spotting the first puddle of puke—mostly beer, with a hint of pretzel—I run into Great Divide founder Brian Dunn and ask how he's doing.

"Drunk," he slurs through his grin. "I was going good for a while but then…" He whistles and makes a downward gesture with his cup.

"I don't think I can do it tonight," I tell him. "Last night was a little rough."

But I do give it one last college try and hasten my sampling. The first hint of a beer buzz, the numb tingle in the mouth and warmth in the belly, doesn't set in until 9:30 or so. I see a young couple lustily pressing their crotches together followed by an older couple playing grab-ass. A sample of coffee-based ale, ten minutes before last call, does me good. I see two Belushi look-alikes in Blues Brothers attire, but no Aykroyd.

I make a misstep when I get a Royal Oil from Denver's Bull and Bush Brewery. It tastes something like strawberry

Mad Dog mixed with chocolate syrup. I don't know if I can get the whole ounce down, but fight my way through the thing just in time to wash away the aftertaste with a last pour of Flying Dog Doppelbock.

On my way out, I see a second puddle of watery pretzel puke. My cup falls out of my pocket, marking the first time it has hit the floor, and the crowd hollers at me just like I hollered at Ingvald the night before.

"Where's my party?" a passing guy asks nobody in particular. He's wearing a top hat crowned by plush beer mugs.

"That was the story of my life last night," I tell him. He ignores me and scans the exiting masses. "Look at all the butts," he says.

Half-full or half-empty?

I catch a train back south and end up sitting next to two middle-aged guys who are wearing the ubiquitous T-shirts identifying them as GABF volunteers. Their name tags are less official, reading "Hugh G. Erection" and "Harry Balsacz." I ask Hugh why he volunteered for the beer fest.

"Free beer," he answers. "And it's fun watching people. The later the night goes, the funner the people are."

Hugh tells me his alter ego is a medical technician at Denver Health. I tell him Duff spent Thursday night in his employer's drunk tank. "Is it pretty busy over there during beer fest weekend?" I ask.

"I'm sure," Hugh replies. "The tech working my shift is going to get hammered—much like her patients." He pauses. "I gotta pee."

Bidding Hugh and Harry good night, I get off at my stop and wander the lonesome industrial alleys of Overland on the walk home, and I'm soon dead to the world in bed, where I remain for a full nine hours.

The next morning, a bit bleary-eyed but in much better shape than either of the previous mornings, I make a run to the local 7-11 to get coffee and cereal. There's a tough-looking drunk at the bus stop, and an older, happier drunk in line in front of me, and yet another drunk who leers at me, grinning, in front of what is perhaps the bleakest dive in Denver, Len & Bill's Bar. It's only three blocks away, but I've drank just about one beer per year there since moving to the neighborhood four years ago.

I finally have some time to catch my breath. I'm skipping the Saturday afternoon session—which includes presenta-tions of the medals and other awards—in order to take care of a growing pile of beer-scented laundry and other house-hold tasks that have taken a backseat to beer for the last few days. But at 3:00 p.m., it's time for more.

I again take the light rail north to downtown, happy to be free of a hangover, this time disembarking beyond the convention center and hoofing it over to the taproom at Great Divide for a quick free sampler. En route, I pass drunks sleeping it off on benches and panhandlers panhandling.

Walking the sidewalk at a fairly brisk clip, I'm following a guy with a backpack who stops and then is following me.

"Fucking Nazis," he says.

I look back. "What?"

"Denver Police," he points to a cop car ahead of us. "Denver is a fascist state."

I tell the guy about Duff two nights earlier.

"There are people in city jail for jaywalking, suit-and-tie people," he responds.

We talk for a couple minutes before I have to turn left, discussing the pure evil of for-profit prisons and making other small talk.

Soon I'm inside the taproom at Great Divide with my four free samples (two I've never tried, Ruffian Barley Wine and Hibernation Ale, as well as two favorites, rice-based Samurai and the Yeti stout). I strike up a conversation with a pair of Israeli guys in town for GABF who are preparing to open a microbrewery back home.

Like it did three days earlier in Fort Collins, a good conversation at a good Colorado taproom keeps me from making it to a second good taproom on my agenda (Flying Dog) before time gets the best of me. I'm starving and have forty-five minutes to walk a half mile, get a bowl of green chili and a pint of Patty's Chile Beer at the bustling Wynkoop Brewing Company—launched in 1988 by Denver Mayor John Hickenlooper—and then run another half mile for volunteer duty at the fest.

I make it with exactly ten seconds to spare, at 5:14:50 p.m.

Fifteen minutes later, I'm behind the merchandise booth, taking orders from other volunteers up front (who are in turn taking orders from the waiting line of people)—"Fat Tire visor!" "Small grey women's PBR shirt!" "Double XL black Ska Brewing sweatshirt!"—then searching through a dozen tables of merchandise and delivering it to said volunteer. They then pass it to the person who originally asked for it. That person then keeps asking for other merch or heads over to the cashier.

It's much more challenging and also much more fun than I expected.

"We retired from drinking," Jill, one of the volunteer crew leaders, tells me. "We absolutely love the event, but we figured the safest bet was to volunteer."

She's got a point.

After hustling for T-shirts and caps until 7:30 with about twenty other volunteers—it's a fairly big operation—I run to the Oskar Blues booth to help pour samples. I immediately discover that this is a much more social duty. When tons of people are coming to you for samples of good beer and you're the one with the pitcher, you sometimes feel pretty cool. I also discover that it's hard to pour exactly an ounce from a pitcher or can.

Working with Marty, Lisa, Chris, and other Oskar Blues friends and family, I trumpet the aged Gordon and crack countless cans of Old Chub and Dale's Pale Ale, also pouring numerous shots of "whatever" and Ten-Fidy. "Whoa," says one guy after his first sip of the latter.

"Yep—it'll put hair on your chest," I tell him.

"I already have hair."

"Then you'll have at least one more."

After ninety minutes of pouring at Oskar Blues, I scramble back to merch to help with the possible end-of-the-fest rush. It's actually pretty mellow. I hone my T-shirt-tossing skills, but my folding skills remain at best remedial.

Another Gordon, please

One funny order stands out. "Okay, he's fairly drunk," a volunteer named Catherine tells me. "He wants a medium of something awesome."

I ask her to clarify.

"He doesn't know what he wants, but it has to be awesome."

I look around and locate a psychedelic tie-dye from Kona Brewing Company in Hawaii and toss it to Catherine. She returns to me a minute later. "He told me I rock and kissed my hand."

At 10 p.m. it's after last call for both beer and T-shirts. I'm stone sober. I didn't have a sip of beer all session long, despite the fact that volunteers are welcome to take beer breaks. But I had a great time, maybe even a better time than when I had an estimated hundred samples. And I got free schwag from the merch booth to boot.

On my way out, I pass a guy with three plates of pizza. "I don't know what we're eating," he says, "but it's good."

I'm writing down that quote as I pass a paid employee at the exit. "Last word," he says, nodding at my pad. "Everybody had fun."

"Yeah?" I ask.

"I didn't see anyone crying," he observes.

Outside, it's a little rainy. I catch my train as I take note of every possible level of sobriety among the passengers. I look at some of the dazed and drunken faces and wonder what is going through their minds.

On my walk home from the Evans light rail station, I decide to stop at the aforementioned Broadway dive, Len & Bill's, for my annual PBR there. En route in the sputtering rain, I have a recollection from the same walk on Thursday night: I passed several police cars parked, red and blues flashing. While a cuffed Duff was being punched by a Denver cop, other Denver cops were manhandling me because they were looking for someone who matched my description: white skin, black shirt, blue cap. I'm amazed I hadn't thought about the incident until three nights later, when the hazy memory jars loose in my head.

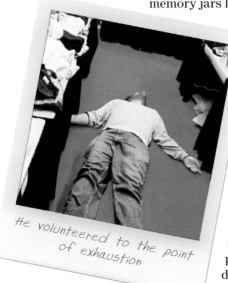

He volunteered to the point of exhaustion

Len & Bill's is as dismal as usual, dusty, poorly maintained, and featuring two drunks at the bar and a drunk bartender behind it. Wynonna Judd is playing on the jukebox.

"Eject this disc!" yells one of the drunks at the bar.

"I'll eject you," says the gruff bartender, who soon mentions to the drunk that she had three shots and a pitcher of beer earlier. The drunk responds by falling asleep at the bar.

At a booth, there's a trio of slumming twenty- and thirty-somethings. The guy asks me if I want to play darts. I reluctantly agree.

He turns out to be a funny guy by the name of Greg and introduces me to his girlfriend, Liesl, and her sister Haley. He tells me he doesn't like beer fest. "I like watery beer, I like to chug it, and I like to pee a lot. How do you mix all those different beers?"

Greg gets me a second PBR, one more than I planned. Before I'm halfway finished, the bartender brings me a

freebie because apparently happy hour never ends at Len & Bill's, no matter how sad the circumstances might be.

We're having fun playing darts by the time that same old beer buzz returns, a tingling partial numbness in my mouth, a nice warm sensation satiating my hungry stomach. Next up, the bloodstream, then the brain, and before long the bladder, as the transformation subtly begins.

Where to go...

Oskar Blues Grill and Brew
303 Main St., Lyons
303-823-6685
www.oskarblues.com

Falling Rock Tap House
1919 Blake St., Denver
303-293-8338
www.fallingrocktaphouse.com

New Belgium Brewing Company
500 Linden St., Fort Collins
888-NBB-4044
www.newbelgium.com

Left Hand Brewing
1265 Boston Ave., Longmont
303-772-0258
www.lefthandbrewing.com

Great American Beer Festival
Held every October in Denver at
the Colorado Convention Center
14th and California Sts., Denver
303-447-0816
www.greatamerican-
beerfestival.com

Old Curtis Street Bar
2100 Curtis St., Denver
303-292-2083

Bar Bar
2060 Champa St., Denver
303-296-1250

3 Kings Tavern
60 S. Broadway, Denver
303-777-7370
www.3kingstavern.net

Denver Police Department
720-913-2000
www.denver.gov/police

Great Divide Brewing Co.
2201 Arapahoe St., Denver
303-296-9640
www.greatdivide.com

Wynkoop Brewing Co.
1634 18th St., Denver
303-297-2700
www.wynkoop.com

Len & Bill's Bar
2301 S. Broadway, Denver
303-722-6484

THE HIGH ROCKIES

INTRODUCTION

This is the mythical Colorado, the amazingly beautiful belt across the state's midsection, just the place to get lost for a day, a week, or a season. Tattooed here and there with mining scars, the rugged, often vertical landscape is as great as any outdoors in the West.

The thin air catalyzes the heady atmosphere, making it easier to get drunk, sexually aroused, and nauseous. (Or all three at once, if you're daring.) With more high points than any state outside of Alaska, Colorado is home to more than fifty fourteeners (14,000-foot peaks, for the uninitiated), which attract far too many people who are in general far too ambitious for my taste. If you want solitude, skip the four-teeners and head to a thirteener or maybe even a twelver.

Demographically speaking, Colorado's High Rockies are a haven for myriad opposing pairs: broke stoners and retired jet-setters, environmentalists and real-estate developers, and Hollywood stars and anonymous illegal immigrants. Average means next to nothing; the billionaires throw the curve too far out of whack.

Up here, skiing is the dominant religion, practiced at resorts such as Steamboat, Vail, and Aspen. Shopping is also big. But things have changed. Take Aspen. In the 1880s, everything revolved around silver. In the 1980s, cocaine had

STATS & FACTS

- Three-quarters of the land over 10,000 feet in the United States is in Colorado.

- Leadville is the country's highest incorporated city, at 10,200 feet above sea level; approximately one-third of the planet's atmosphere is below you.

- With more than 12 million "skier days" annually, Colorado's ski industry is by far the largest of any state, about twice the size of second-place California's.

- The dinky town of Marble is named for its main industry: This is where the marble for the Colorado State Capitol, the Lincoln Memorial, and the Tomb of the Unknown Soldier originated. It's also great for cheap souvenirs, which can be dug out from a box of snow-white marble chips at the mill. The suggested donation is a buck a pound.

- When listed by its Saudi prince owner in 2006, the ninety-five-acre compound north of Aspen known as "Hala" touted a fifteen-bedroom, 56,000-square-foot mansion, and set a real-estate record with the asking price of a whopping $135 million.

taken its place. By 2080, who knows? Beachfront property might be the latest Aspen craze, if earthquakes and global warming shear off and sink everything to the west.

But not every mountain has been sold to the highest bidder: Plenty of them remain pristine and protected, in the form of Rocky Mountain National Park, in addition to several national forests and wilderness areas. There are more elk living in Colorado in than any other state, some 300,000 of them. The mountain lions are enjoying a smorgasbord.

All things considered, the rocky wonderland running along the spine of the state is just the place to get lost for a good long while. The thin air, sin-enhancing side effects and all, will do you good.

BIG THINGS AND OTHER ROAD ART

Guffey
26 miles south of Hartsel via CO 9
www.guffeycolorado.com

The extra mileage off the beaten path is a small price to pay to check out Guffey (pop. 30) for an hour or two. Bill Soux, the proprietor of the Guffey Garage, Last Chance Antiques, and several rental cabins in town, is also a mad

artist. His masterpieces: the exterior of the Guffey Garage (which looks like a cross between a Wild West barroom, Dr. Frankenstein's lab, and a psychedelic vision) and across the street the ominous "Prison Wagon," a mannequin jailbird in a cell atop a wagon pulled by the skeletal remains of two horses and driven by a human skeleton. Soux's cabins are also funky and historic, and cheap

Read:

- Anything by former Woody Creek resident Hunter S. Thompson

Listen:

- The unofficial Colorado State song (and ode to smoking marijuana at elevation) "Rocky Mountain High," by former Woody Creek resident (and Thompson neighbor) John Denver

Watch:

- South Park, Dumb and Dumber, The Shining

To-Do Checklist:

- Get as high as you can

- Ski naked

- Be one with nature (don't forget toilet paper—and pack it out)

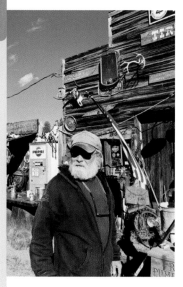

($35–$55 for two), and his imagination runs wild in all sorts of directions. He is the proud owner of Guffey's mayor, a black cat named Monster who is the latest in a long line of pets to pull the strings in town, and the mastermind behind the annual Fourth of July Chicken Fly, where kids with plungers goad chickens from a mailbox and see how far they fly before touching down. The record is sixty feet.

Steve Canyon Statue
Colorado Blvd. and Miner St., Idaho Springs

Dedicated to all men and women who served the United States in uniform, this statue is not of an actual man or woman who served the United States in uniform, but in fact is a fictional man who served in a fictional uniform in the funny pages, Steve Canyon. Written and illustrated by Milton Caniff from 1947 to 1988, Steve Canyon was memorialized by Idaho Springs in the form of a limestone likeness commissioned by the local chamber of commerce in 1950 to drum up publicity for the gateway mountain town.

Chrome Dragon and Knight
Town Park, Crested Butte

Sculptor Sean Guerrero's preferred medium is chrome—plated car bumpers—and his subject matter tends toward the fantastic.

Some of his best-known work has been a roadside attraction in Crested Butte for years: a dragon and knight locked in mortal combat. Typically, the dragon is on the dark side and the knight is aligned with the good guys, but this being the site of Vinotok—where the knight is annually vanquished by the Earth Dragon in the perpetual clash between technology and nature—I'll put my money on the dragon.

R.I.P.

Hunter S. Thompson, 1937–2005
Owl Farm, Woody Creek

Hunter S. Thompson was a mad wizard of words, ramped up on all sorts of potions and pills and powders, spinning tales that inspired scads of drug-fueled expeditions to Vegas, Aspen, and everywhere else.

Few writers leave an entire genre as their legacy like Thompson did with gonzo journalism. Especially when espousing politics or fury or, at his best, both, his grammatical alchemy—equal parts substance-propelled introspection, skewed reportage, and verbal pyrotechnics—will be worth reading as long as English is in circulation.

A 150-foot monument dubbed the "Gonzo Memorial Fist" was unveiled in August 2005; the monument doubled as a cannon that blasted Thompson's ashes all over the property. The two-thumbed hand (holding an upturned mushroom) was financed through the sale of a special-edition beer and donations from the Hollywood elite. But Aspen's finicky ruling class eventually forced the estate to take it down; at press time, it was on mothballs.

So the best way to pay your respects to the good doctor is probably hoisting a Molson at Woody Creek Tavern, his onetime local haunt.

Cannibal Plateau
**About 10 miles northeast
of Lake City**

This is where convicted cannibal Alfred "Alferd" Packer allegedly ate four of his buddies after a hellacious storm in the winter of 1874. While the truth is disputed to this day—Packer was eventually pardoned and died a vegetarian—there is no doubt his traveling party met terrible deaths here.

Burros: Prunes and Shorty
Front St. and Main St. (respectively), Fairplay

Fairplay's two most famous graves are the final resting places for two very different burros: Prunes, a hardworking miner's helper who lived more than sixty years, and Shorty, who was said to be lazier than Prunes but beloved by Fairplayers nonetheless. What about the third most famous grave in town? That would be Bum, a dog who was Shorty's best friend.

VICE

Minturn Saloon
146 Main St., Minturn
970-827-5954

A rare ski-in bar in a town—at least for now—without a resort, the Minturn is best known for its margaritas. The après-ski party-hardy atmosphere is second. Somewhere further down the list is the food: The quail enchiladas are the specialty, but anything tastes okay after three of the margs.

Woody Creek Tavern
Upper River Rd., Woody Creek
970-923-4585

You can't ski into the place, but the margaritas at the Woody Creek blow away the Minturn's. And the food isn't even in the same culinary universe: Spicy but not over-whelmingly so, it's Mexican with a Colorado twist, plus stellar bar food. But most folks come here to pay tribute to Dr. Gonzo himself, Hunter S. Thompson, Woody Creek's most famous resident even in death. The tavern was his local haunt, at least until it got overrun with aspiring writers who used to hassle him to no end while the man tried to enjoy his booze and his night.

Wheel Bar
132 E. Elkhorn Ave., Estes Park
970-586-9381

Open every day except Christmas since 1945, the Wheel Bar is a one-of-a-kind: Estes Park's oldest and rowdiest watering hole, with a strangely hypnotic wheel rotating behind the bar. Opened by Orlando Nagl and still operated by the Nagl family, this joint has a long and storied history as the town's de facto bank, gambling den, and pretty much everything else you can imagine in its sixty-plus-year history. Attracting tourists and locals alike, the Wheel is the best spot for a post-backpacking bender after going walkabout in Rocky Mountain National Park.

Ullr Fest
Breckenridge
www.gobreck.com

The Norse god of snow, Ullr, is known for his mad skiing and archery skills, but he must have a fondness for beer as well: Breckenridge's annual Ullr Fest is as much about the bar scene as it is about the ski slopes. With drink specials and nightly events that straddle the line between Vice and Huh?—the latter exemplified by Ullympics (which include the frying pan toss) and a parade (which includes hot tubs on wheels)—the weeklong paean is the nation's most popular ski town's way of paying tribute to the deity who not only frosts the local slopes with 300 inches of white stuff annually, but also apparently loves a good party.

Ice Bar
On the mountain, Crested Butte
970-349-2275

Bellying up to a bar made of ice isn't as cold on your stomach as you'd think, especially if you've had a few après-ski rounds beforehand. On the mountain, this bar sadly melts like Frosty come springtime, but it's a solid place to get a drink during the ski season.

STAR MAPS

While I've had my share of fun in Aspen, I think it's time to let Beverly Hills annex it. The ritziest ski town the world has ever seen has much more in common with California's most posh 'hoods than it does with geographic neighbors like Basalt and Leadville. And it's got enough movie stars to make you sick.

The futuristic house in Woody Allen's sci-fi send-up *Sleeper* is located in Genesee, visible from I-70.

In *Dumb and Dumber*, Harry and Lloyd's expedition to Aspen, "where the beer flows like wine," is one of the most sidesplitting road movies ever, but in fact Aspen proved far too pricey a location so Estes Park served as its double. Other great *Dumb* Colorado-related moments include Lloyd accidentally heading east at the Nebraska state line and Harry, noting, "John Denver was full of shit."

The eponymous town in the TV cartoon *South Park*, created by former Colorado residents Trey Parker and Matt Stone, is said to be loosely based on Fairplay.

HUH?

Great Stupa
of Dharmakaya
Which Liberates
Upon Seeing
4921 County Rd. 68C, Red Feather Lakes
888-788-7221
www.shambhalamountain.org

As the eleventh reincarnation in a line of Tibetan Buddhist masters, Chogyam Trungpa Rinpoche was one of the prime catalysts behind the Tibetan Buddhism boom in the U.S.

during the 1970s. He was also something of a drunken lech.

Trungpa's skull is entombed for eternity inside a massive Buddha statue that sits lotus-style in a massive *stupa*—a towering spire serving as a monument to a great Buddhist teacher like old Trungpan himself. As a matter of fact, Trungpa, who died at the age of forty-seven in 1987 with a bum liver, is still so beloved to this day that the stupa his followers built is the largest in the Western Hemisphere: The Great Stupa of Dharmakaya Which Liberates Upon Seeing (heretofore referred to in this text as T.G.S.O.D.W.L.U.S.) is 108 feet tall and one of the most ornate and durable structures you'll find in the middle of nowhere anywhere.

Built over the course of thirteen years at the Shambhala Mountain Center (with additional panels continually in progress), T.G.S.O.D.W.L.U.S. may or may not liberate your consciousness at first sight, but it will almost certainly impress. Laden with multihued panels crafted by the most patient and skilled of craftsman, the stupa was built to stand for 1,000 years. It follows that the folks who engineered it specialize in nuclear facilities, utilizing concrete and miles of rebar.

Now T.G.S.O.D.W.L.U.S. is the visual centerpiece of the center, which offers a year-round curriculum focusing on meditation, yoga, and the teachings of Trungpa. Tent-cabins, hiking trails, and a meditation center round out the campus. Buddhists and non-Buddhists alike are welcome to visit or bunk down for the night.

Devil's Thumb
**Indian Peaks Wilderness Area,
northeast of Fraser**

After years of bloody warfare, the Arapaho and the Ute
tribes were finally ready to bury the figurative hatchet, so
they buried the devil himself for good measure. And not the
Christian devil (a.k.a. Satan, Lucifer, or Beelzebub) nor Dick
Cheney, but the real devil: violence. They stopped fighting,
and to remind themselves not to start again—because fighting
never resulted in anything but injury, death, and sadness—
they kept the devil's thumb sticking out of the mountain.
Then the white man came up and Anglicized the original
moniker into Devil's Thumb. The devil remains buried, but
he's been hitchhiking ever since, and unfortunately I think
he may have gotten a ride but left his thumb behind to fool us
naïve Coloradans.

Vinotok
**Every Fall Equinox, Crested Butte
www.cbweekly.com**

"Burn the Grump!" I yell. "Burn it!"

In the heart of Crested Butte, hundreds of people gather
for the annual trial of the Grump. After locals—dressed in
odd medieval-looking costumes—dance, sing, and booze their
way through every eating and drinking establishment on Elk
Avenue, hundreds mass in the center of town for the trial. First
comes the "infinite" battle between the knight, "representing
technology...the molybdenum mine," and the Earth Dragon,
"representing nature, people, good fortune, and everything
wild." The dragon makes short work of the knight, the audience
cheers, but then the Green Man—a local dressed in green with
a crown of green leaves and green face paint—begins to suffer
onstage. He is dying. After a smattering of debate, it is decided
the Grump must take the Green Man's place.

"Burn the Grump!"

Then the crowd of hundreds follows the Grump—a twenty-foot-tall fearsome effigy of the attendees' problems and grievances, complete with a horse-skull head, wings, and glowing red eyes—which is placed in the center of an unlit bonfire. A few moments later, the Grump is gone and the bonfire rages. My girlfriend, Ruthie, and I chuck our written grievances into the fire (mine include global warming, greed, monkey-killers, and conga lines). A drunken fellow we encountered earlier asks me to hold his PBR while he sneaks through the partition for a victory lap around the flames. "That was sick" he says as I hand him back his can.

Loosely based on Slovenian traditions, Vinotok is a debauched and joyful event; locals drop their written griev-ances into boxes in town to be burned with the Grump. The bonfire was once open to anyone throwing on it anything else they wanted to burn—old skis, TV sets, etc.—but that was toned down for obvious reasons. Ultimately, the locals are at once saying goodbye to the green summer and embracing the white winter—and throwing a hell of a bash in the process.

"The party's over," I crack to the guy cleaning up beer bottles around the parking lot the next morning.

"Nah," he replies. "It's just getting started."

Ice Palace Park
W. 10th St., Leadville

Local leaders were looking for a tourist lure after the silver market crashed in 1893, so they built a fabulous Ice Palace, indeed the word's largest frozen castle, in 1896. Ornate and over the top (complete with a skating rink, fine dining, and a grand ballroom), the concept went bust after an early spring turned the thing to slush in May. The spot where the town's dreams began to melt away—Leadville's modern population of about 2,500 is down more than 90 percent from its 1880s peak of 50,000—is now commemorated by a nondescript city park.

Old Man Mountain
West of Estes Park

The site of countless vision quests—walkabouts in the woods
in search of a vision—Old Man Mountain holds the mythical
key to understanding one's place in the universe. The mountain
(which bears a resemblance to a seated man if you squint at it
just right) has been frequented by native peoples on spiritual
quests for thousands of years and remains as good a place as
any to find the answer to that question you've been asking yourself over and over and over again.

GRUB

K. K.'s BBQ
The Center of the Universe, Rancho Del Rio
4199 Trough Rd., Bond
970-653-4431
www.ranchodelrio.com

K. K. is my favorite chef in Colorado,
although I've only eaten at her place a
couple of times. Her outdoor barbecue
joint on the Colorado River serves all
sorts of delicacies made of expertly
grilled meat, plus sundaes and serve-
yourself cans of beer. (K. K. keeps tabs,
as do customers, then they compare them
when it comes time to settle up.) But the
true magic comes from K. K.'s incom-
parable wit. She tells dirty jokes, rings
bells to commemorate just about everything, and has comebacks galore. When
folks complain about her prices, K. K.
tells them, "Why don't you go across the
street?" The unspoken punch line: There
isn't another restaurant for miles.

Original Hard Rock Cafe
18 E. Park Ave., U.S. 40, Empire
303-569-2618

This woodsy diner was established in 1934 to serve hard-rock miners, thirty-seven years before the first Hard Rock Café went up. When the chain came to Colorado, the place deservedly staved off a lawsuit over the moniker. (I guess the Dairy King down the street wasn't so lucky.) Not only is this Hard Rock's T-shirt more unique than the ubiquitous ones from the other Hard Rocks, this is a better place to eat, with a basic menu for breakfast and lunch that includes pancakes, omelets, burritos, and burgers.

Coney Island
10 Old Stagecoach Rd., Bailey
303-838-4210

Coney Island is a fourteen-ton hot dog moving southwest at an average speed of about 1.3 miles a year since it first opened on West Colfax in Denver in 1966. The original owner—who patented his design and hoped to franchise the concept nationwide—left the restaurant a few years later, and the shuttered fake frankfurter was put on wheels and shipped forty miles down U.S. 285. Things went smoothly in the country until Denver's exurbs encroached, and again the big concrete wiener got on a truck and moved farther southwest, fifteen more miles down U.S. 285, this time to Bailey. Not surprisingly, the culinary focus is hot dogs, but the shakes and malts alone are worth a stop by the creek.

MISC.

Rancho Del Rio
**4199 Trough Rd., near the headwaters
of the Colorado River, Bond
970-653-4431
www.ranchodelrio.com**

One of the last of a breed of ramshackle rafting communities, Rancho Del Rio is a river rat's paradise, a place where you can paddle all day and party all night, then sleep in your car in the parking lot. A half-dozen operations offer guided rafting trips, and the Colorado River Center (888-888-RAFT, www.coloradorivercenter.com) also offers guided kayaking excursions as well as rentals of all kinds. Shuttles are available to pick you up and carry you and your craft back to Rancho, where you can meditate over your amazing day on the river over a cold beer and a burger at K. K.'s BBQ.

Ultimate Taxi
**Aspen and vicinity
970-927-9239
www.ultimatetaxi.com**

One of the few appropriate uses of the word *ultimate*, Jon Barnes's Ultimate Taxi is a 1978 Checker cab done up in, um, ultimate style. For the passengers' listening pleasure, the taxi also has an incredible sound system and Jon plays a synthesizer and a crazy computerized woodwind en route to your destination. For the passengers' visual pleasure, there are miles of fiber-optic filaments, laserlights, and complimentary 3-D glasses. For good measure, the taxi has a roller coaster simulator on the dash that can induce motion sickness among drunks at a mere five miles per hour, and it also has webcams that immortalize its buzzed riders online. (The best of the site's archives is a video of Hunter S. Thompson in 1990, philosophically waxing, "Yesterday's weirdness is tomorrow's reason why.") The fare isn't cheap—$150— but Barnes is the best person to call for a lift if you don't have a destination in mind and are in no hurry to get there.

Strawberry Park Hot Springs Resort

44200 County Rd. 36, Steamboat Springs
970-879-0342
www.strawberryhotsprings.com

My personal favorite of all of Colorado's commercialized hot springs, Strawberry Park is a soaker's paradise, with a series of hot pools cut into the forest with a very bohemian feel. The resort, accessible via road or trail, is fed by the 150-degrees-Fahrenheit hot springs that intermingle with cooler creek waters in a series of pools that top out at 104 degrees. After hours, the hot springs is open only to guests in the cabins, yurts, and restored caboose (complete with a kitchenette and gas fireplace), and the swimsuits-required policy is relaxed.

Leadville Equine Skijoring

First weekend in March, Leadville

Every year since the 1940s, Harrison Avenue—the main drag in Leadville—is turned into a frosty obstacle course with truckloads of snow from nearby Turquoise Lake. The big event—skijoring—involves horses towing skiers at speeds of thirty miles an hour down the street over several jumps. The skiers need to navigate the course and grab several hanging rings—not unlike a vintage carousel—as they pass. The ancient bars on Harrison are full of activity as locals place bets on the teams in between beers.

If skijoring sounds a bit unsafe, that's probably because it is—I saw a horse fall down on its rider near the finish line one year—but it's probably no more dangerous than the slopes at nearby Copper Mountain or the Denver Broncos playing football.

Rocky Mountain National Park
West of Estes Park
970-586-1206
www.nps.gov/romo

I've taken dozens of day hikes in Rocky Mountain National Park and traversed Trail Ridge Road a comparable number of times. It never gets old (well, unless you get caught behind an RV), this mostly untouched mountain wonderland with an amazing sixty peaks topping out over 12,000 feet above sea level. A third of the park is above treeline, bleakly beautiful alpine tundra with beautiful forested valleys, babbling brooks, and idyllic meadows below. But visitors are missing the point if they stick to the pavement. This is a hiker's park, first and foremost, with more than 350 miles of trails begging for your boots.

World's Largest Organism?
Atop Kebler Pass, northwest of Crested Butte

When you look at a mountainside turned into a vibrant sea of color by the resident stands of quaking aspens, you aren't looking at a forest of trees, but typically just a few organisms. Scores of genetically identical aspen share one root structure, which is what makes them turn color all at once. Because of this, scientists consider the largest aspen stands in the Rockies to be among the world's largest organisms. While Utah has claimed it too has the world's largest organism, Colorado's contender for the title is on top of Kebler Pass, 9,980 feet above sea level, and weighing tens of thousands of tons—although aspen groves are notoriously difficult to weigh.

Colorado Trail
Denver to Durango
www.coloradotrail.org

By paved road, the route from Denver to Durango is 336 miles—you can make it there in six or seven hours. But if you've got more time (a lot more time), take the Colorado Trail, which runs about 480 miles between the two cities. By foot, the trip usually takes more than a month, although one especially energetic fellow zipped over it in just two weeks, sustaining himself on a diet of vegetable oil and multivitamins. The trail starts at Waterton Canyon southwest of Denver at about 6,000 feet above sea level and ends near

Durango at an elevation of about 7,000 feet, but it climbs a mind-boggling total of 77,690 feet (and drops 76,210 feet) in the process.

But don't feel compelled to undertake the entire journey (I haven't). There are a number of access points near mountain towns that allow for great day hikes on the trail. And if you are feeling like a week of hard but rewarding labor in the back-country, you can sign up for a volunteer trail crew and help reverse the ravages of snowmelt. Some volunteers sign up for multiple crews, which is one of the cheapest ways to sustain yourself in the Rockies for a summer: One $50 fee covers all of your meals for every day you volunteer, all summer long.

A CHIMP RIDING A UNICYCLE: A SKIING VIRGIN HITS THE SLOPES

3 DAYS, 230 MILES (PLUS PLENTY OF SKI RUNS AND WIPEOUTS)

On the way to Utah last weekend, I drove by Vail, Loveland, and the other Colorado ski resorts strung along I-70. More than once, my glance went sideways to watch the insect-sized skiers riding the lifts up and squiggling their way down. The slopes looked really steep.

I was once scared of heights but conquered my acrophobia at age ten or so. The cure involved leaping from the high dive at the Woodmoor Country Club's pool until realizing the pool would always catch me. Ten years later, I went snorkeling in the Cayman Islands' Stingray City and found mingling with the rays to be a very visceral way of confronting one's fear. So was diving in the shark tank at the Denver aquarium another decade or so later.

What am I most afraid of? Easy answer: the unknown.

Not that I'm unique in my vague dread of the strange and unfamiliar. The fear of the unknown must be the most common, all-encompassing phobia of all, since it overlaps with thanatophobia, the fear of the scariest of all unknown quantities—death—and many others, like, for instance, skiing, which is a great big unknown to me.

The fact that I've never skied before is strange to most strangers, because I was born and raised in Colorado and still live in Denver. Writing from experience, one of the most common introductory questions asked of a Colorado native is, "Do you ski?" I'm now in my mid-thirties, and people have surely posed that question to me several hundred times.

And to date, I've always answered them, "No. Actually, I've never skied. No, not even once in my entire life."

Then I'd often mention that many native New Yorkers have never been up in the Empire State Building and many native Memphians have never been to Graceland. I also have used my non-skiing parents as an excuse. It just isn't in my blood, I'd say.

Numerous people I've met over the years have simply assumed I was an expert skier once they heard the magic word *Colorado*, which is synonymous with skiing to so many ears. But to me, Colorado has always just been home, slopes or no slopes, and skiing has been something for tourists or ski bums or jocks, but not for me.

Lately, however, I've searched for a reason why I've avoided the slopes all these years, and the best root cause I've come up with is fear of the unknown. And the only way to truly conquer the fear of the unknown is to confront it and make it known. Sure, I'm also afraid of breaking a leg or a spine or any and every breakable thing in my body, but that seems remote if I stick to beginners' lessons and bunny hills on the excursion I'm embarking on tomorrow morning: my first ski trip, only thirty-four years and fifty days (and approximately 572 "Do you ski?" queries) after my birth in Colorado Springs, 1973.

· · · · ·

On my ninety-minute drive from Denver to old mining town and current ski and snowboarding mecca Breckenridge, the butterflies grow increasingly restless. It doesn't help that I have to pee. I'm as nervous as I've been in a long time.

My fearless instructor Roman

The bustling base lodge is totally alien to me. I look around at the masses gearing up and making beelines to the lifts. Myself, I have to rent gear, so I first go through the hectic rental process and commandeer boots, skis, poles, and a helmet. The last accessory is optional, but I figure it can't hurt.

I'm soon paired with Roman Bodnar, my instructor in Breckenridge's "Learn to Ski" program. He sizes me up and says, "We're going to have some fun today."

I confess about my nervousness. "Fear is normal," he responds, easing my trepidation with his Zen-like calm and absolute mastery of skiing backwards.

We start at the bunny hill. Roman teaches me to take the ready pose and to hold my arms forward and to pivot my feet. Piece of cake. He emphasizes balance, noting, "Your body balances better than your mind or eyes think it can." He also tells me that it takes 1,000 repetitions of just about every skiing move before your muscles memorize it.

I learn the defensive skiing position known as the wedge, or the snowplow, knock-kneed, ski tips together, used to slow down or stop. I embrace it as a shield against my terror. It quickly becomes my next move.

I graduate from the bunny hill in no time, and we move to the Poma lift for a couple of short runs. I obviously get high marks on those, too, because we are quickly on the real chairlift, heading up to a novice green slope, one of the resort's flattest and much tamer than the intermediate blues or expert blacks.

On the way up, Roman tells about ten skiing jokes. Among them: "What do you call a snowboarder in a coat and tie? The defendant." "How many Vail ski instructors does it take to put in a light bulb? Just one—he just stands there and holds the bulb, and the world revolves around him."

Our first trip down is marked by me forgetting everything Roman taught me and wiping out several times. We take the trail marked "EASIEST WAY DOWN," and I manage to get back to the base in one piece, albeit eating the dust of numerous toddlers and just about every other demographic.

So we ascend again, and I ask Roman about the Ukrainian hometown listed on his name tag. He explains that his true birthplace—a displaced persons camp in Stuttgart, Germany—has nothing to do with his heritage. His father was a Ukrainian who got forced into a Nazi labor camp but met Roman's mother at the aforementioned camp after World War II.

Upon Roman's birth, the family immigrated to Canada and soon made a home in Rochester, New York.

Roman, now in his fifties, also tells me that he's "reinventing himself" after a career in retail. A skier since childhood, he's now a full-time ski instructor and a part-time personal trainer. He gives me a business card for the latter profession that showcases his shirtless, buff chest.

After lunch—I'm famished—my second run down is much more successful. I keep my hands forward, I stand tall, I turn, and I don't wipe out.

"Congratulations," says Roman. "You're a skier!"

I smile and soon wipe out again. But I've definitely made strides.

We make a few more runs. Roman must bark the refrain "Stand tall! Arms forward!" about a hundred times. When I follow his advice, I am a skier. When I don't, I'm anything but, like on our attempt to take the steeper alternative to the "EASIEST WAY DOWN." This route results in me not standing tall, wildly swinging my poles, and falling down several times.

As it nears 4 p.m.—closing time for the lifts—we make a foray into a terrain park. I make it over one mound of snow, but crash on the second. I have trouble pushing myself to my feet because of sheer exhaustion, and struggling to push myself up makes me that much more exhausted. I feebly finish the run, my circulatory system struggling to figure out what hit it.

The lifts are still open as I limp to the base. Roman doesn't want this debacle to be the end to my first day of skiing, but I'm actually fine with it. Fear has taken a backseat to fatigue.

After checking in at my hotel—the Lodge & Spa at Breckenridge, perched on a mountainside high above town—and taking a shower, I meet Roman for a couple of local microbrews at his home away from home, the Schussbaumer Ski Club's chalet. While he lives near Denver, he spends four nights a week on a bunk in a dorm here during the ski season.

He pays just $495 in annual dues for that privilege—which averages to $4 a night for him—in addition to $50 for all the keg beer he can drink. On this night, he's got the place pretty much to himself.

We recount my first day on the slopes. Roman says that I conquered my fear on the gentler terrain, but it took the reins on the steeper stuff. I concur.

"But you progressed very well," he adds.

The conversation turns back toward fear. "What initially is fear," Roman sagely notes, "eventually turns to thrill."

We discuss the fact that I'll be out the next day with a different instructor at a different resort—Copper Mountain—and how that will affect my learning curve. He says it might be preferable to continue with him on the same slope for two more days. I agree, but my lesson at Copper is already scheduled.

Tips up!

His parting advice: "Stand tall!"

All in all, the day made my most common phobia that much more irrelevant. The fear isn't gone, not yet, but I believe I'll sleep much more soundly tonight, the knot in my right buttock notwithstanding. After a microwave pizza and a Gatorade—I didn't quite feel up to a bar and/or grill—I go to bed.

· · · · ·

For whatever reason, I snooze for only five or six of my nine horizontal hours and still feel bruised and beaten when I wake at 7 a.m. My fear nearly immediately flares at the brief thought of careening out of control down a ski slope. Before once and for all abandoning the bed for the day, I momentarily wish I had a time machine so I could stay in it for eight more hours or so. Alas, I do not.

But coffee and breakfast do me good. Unfortunately, I'm running a few minutes behind and that percolates my nervousness for no good reason. The fear is still with me.

I'm punctual after all, making it to the Center Village in Copper Mountain—owned by ski industry behemoth Intrawest—with time to spare before my group of six beginners sets out for the day. Our fearless leader is Dennis Meeker, a ski instructor for thirty-three years and Copper Mountain's newly crowned "2006–2007 Instructor of the Year."

"If it's not fun, you're doing something wrong," Dennis emphasizes right off the bat.

I ask about the hobby, "ROCK & ROLL," mentioned on his name tag.

"It used to be blank, blank, and ROCK & ROLL," he laughs. I guess corporate America has no sense of humor.

On our first run, Dennis sizes up each skier in the group, advising us on our strengths and weaknesses. Most everyone except me is from sea level. We are all at the same relative skill level. Several in the group are on the slopes for their second day ever.

While some of my fear remains, my fatigue evaporates on contact with adrenaline. I make some mistakes but don't topple. Dennis takes note of the same tendencies Roman highlighted: crouching, leaning, and holding my arms to my sides instead of in front of me.

Compared with the slope I was on at Breckenridge, our run off the Kokomo lift is relatively crowd-free. The extra space does a lot for my focus and calm. I'm not worried about getting run over by a snowboarder or running over a three-year-old. There are plenty of both, but we've all got room to operate.

The kids amaze me. Some who must have learned to walk mere months ago are zipping down the mountain without apprehension. "For them, it's playing," Dennis says on a chairlift ride up. "For adults, the perception is, it's dangerous."

I should try to be more like a toddler on my next run, I think. Except for the pants-wetting, that is.

We focus on our turns and feeling our rotary motion on our skis on the next trip down. Once again, I make it without serious incident. My nervousness is diminishing significantly since the early flare-up.

Dennis usually leads our group down the hill, stopping two or three times to offer pointers and tips to each of us. "Skiing is not stopping," he says, encouraging the group to speed up. "If you have a vintage '68 Ferrari, is it funner to drive it or look at it?"

I've never driven a '68 Ferrari, but I assume, like with my '01 Saturn, it's more fun to drive one than look at one. Dennis assures us this is the case.

After lunch, we start opening the wedge, speeding up, and working on parallel skiing. Loping down the slope in long, wide turns feels better and better. Speed no longer equals terror. I'm able to get a little bit of that toddleresque Zen and ski without feeling the need to stop or crouch or lean. Well, I still lean in one direction or another too much, trying to steer or stop with my upper half.

But I make strides with every run and start to truly learn the lessons Roman tried to instill in me right off the bat yesterday: Stay loose, use your upper body as only a balance, and do the work with your legs. My center of gravity starts to feel like a natural pendulum as I shift my weight from one foot to the other and back again. It's controlled chaos, I think, with the slope being the chaos and my innate balance the control.

The hell of ski traffic

"You're skiing!" Dennis yells to the entire group. It's clear we've all made strides in our short period together, our collective confidence beginning to eclipse our collective fear.

On the chair up for our final run of the day, I tell Dennis I'm pleased that I haven't fallen today, because pushing myself back up from the ground was by far the most tiring aspect of my trip thus far.

He tells me that fatigue was normal for a "snow virgin," but it's not normal for the sport. "Skiing isn't work. It doesn't require muscular effort to get the job done."

"You ever go on a blind date and absolutely hate the person, and then they wear on you?" he adds. "Yesterday was your blind date."

I tell him I never hated my blind date, I was just a little scared of her.

The next run down is my best one yet. My wipeout tally for all of day two still stands at zero. (I almost fell in the lift line once, but managed to recover.) I feel I've made significant progress.

While not exhausted, I still feel some fatigue—particularly in my feet muscles—and elect to head back to Breckenridge for the night instead of attempting my first solo run. Maybe I'll try it tomorrow after my morning lesson at Loveland.

I head back to the hotel for a couple hours of rest and vegetation, but hunger eventually forces me to take the hotel shuttle into downtown Breckenridge, two miles and 250 feet below, for dinner.

I'm dropped off at the Breckenridge Brewery, but the lack of barstool vacancies compels me to Downstairs at Eric's, a longtime après-ski haunt laden with stickers and arcade games, past the bistros and boutiques down the street.Maybe I've warmed up to skiing, I think en route, but my jury's still out to resort towns. After dinner and a couple of beers, however, I'm swayed to contentedness as I stare at a red, white, and blue sticker reading "An eagle can't fly on just a right wing."

After the shuttle returns me to my room, I sleep well for the first night in three.

I awaken to several inches of fresh snow. I have break- fast, pack up, and head to Loveland for my last day of ski lessons. Feeling a sense of calm as I drive seventy miles per hour on a wet highway, I think of one of Dennis's com- ments the afternoon before: "You've heard of white-knuckle driving? There's also white-knuckle skiing."

Despite my speed and the weather this early spring morning, I'm not white-knuckle driving. Sure, driving has been second nature to me for nearly twenty years, whereas skiing is not yet second nature to me at all. To make it so, the same inner calm is critical. I take a deep breath, feeling good.

After driving under Loveland Pass via the Johnson Tunnel on eastbound I-70, I park at Loveland at about 9:30. The long-standing ski area features plenty of locally beloved terrain but little in the way of development: no hotels, no boutiques, no oxygen bars, just a few eateries, watering holes, and rental shops. I like the bare-bones setup immedi- ately, especially the notable lack of a horde.

The resort is divided into Loveland Basin and Loveland Valley. My two-and-a-half-hour morning lesson is at the latter, under the tutelage of longtime ski instructor Don Davidson, sporting a bald head, grey beard, and golden earring. The class is just me and one other novice student,

T. D., a middle-aged woman from Minnesota. It is snowing when I get there and continues to do so off and on all day.

On our first chairlift ride up, Don asks me, "What is skiing?"

"It's, uh, balancing your body so you can use gravity, um, to navigate yourself down the slope of the terrain," I struggle.

"Skiing is walking downhill," he coolly replies.

Thus, on our first run down the short, crowd-free bunny hill, we walk while skiing, taking little steps to our right and left to demonstrate their effect on our respective trajectories. A small step to the left steers me left, and, since left is uphill, I decelerate and come to a stop right next to Don.

Next we work on abandoning the wedge in favor of straightening out our skis and using our lower half for steering and our upper half for balance. Don emphasizes that you have to adjust your balance according to the steepness of the slope. "You can't be a tree," he says, crossing his poles at the angle of a tree on a hill. He makes them perpendicular. "You've got to be a skier."

At one point, Don threatens us mildly with remedial action if we don't stop snowplowing. We eventually leave our poles at the bottom, and both T. D. and I make progress on our ability to steer by shifting our balance from foot to foot and gently turning our skis.

Halfway down the hill, Don pulls us aside for some pointers. "Imagine you're a chimpanzee riding a unicycle," he says.

This ridiculous mental image grabs me immediately.

He explains how skiers need to maintain steady chimp-like postures with their arms, shoulders, and upper body for balance, while steering with their ankles, hips, and knees as if they were riding a unicycle.

I nod. This is exactly what I need: the opportunity to picture myself as a circus monkey.

Don skis ahead, gaining speed as gravity grabs him, and then goes into a perfectly circular arc across the slope. As he completes a 180-degree turn, he sails uphill until gravity counteracts his momentum and brings him to a stop.

I follow, steering my left ski left with my little toe and my right ski left with my big toe, all while standing tall and keeping my arms ahead. The picture of a helmeted chimp on a unicycle speeding down the snow enters my head as I zoom across an arc very similar to Don's.

"Great!" he says. "You just made your first parallel turn!"

I think of the chimp on the unicycle and do it again. Maybe I really am a skier. Nonetheless, Don advises me to stick to Loveland Valley in the afternoon.

After my lesson with Don ends, I leave my skis behind and take the shuttle to meet my friend Doug Ottke at the bar at Loveland Basin. Doug, who's skied since he was a kid, buys me a beer, and I tell him about my skiing experience thus far.

"I'm not skiing over here on this mountain," I add, noting Don's advice. "I'm only going to ski at the other one on the easy green run. I want to practice my turns for a while."

Doug says he thinks I should at least do one run at Loveland Basin. "That way, you can get a feel for the whole resort."

I'm hesitant. He decides to take the shuttle back over and ski the Basin's bunny hill with me. After two easy spins down, Doug is certain I'm ready for a long green run, with a touch of intermediate blue, on the other mountain. I decide to give it a shot.

Soon we're getting off the chairlift above timberline (12,038 feet above sea level) at Loveland Basin. Snow is falling and mixing with the clouds and sun and rock and trees to form an otherworldly, beautiful landscape.

It looks a little steeper (and a lot more crowded) than the bunny hill, but I'm convinced I can handle it. I'm a skier now, after all.

"The first part is the hardest," says Doug as he pushes off. "Don't get discouraged."

I follow confidently in the same direction, but just as the word *discouraged* vanishes into the wintry air, I'm falling on my ass, losing a ski in the process.

I must've done something wrong. I struggle down after Doug, who patiently waits a short distance below.

Soon there is a stretch of steeper intermediate-blue terrain ahead, which Doug instinctively zips down.

I stop and look down in horror. "It's too steep!" I yell. No response. I slowly push off and go into the first of many parallel turns. Fear quickly eclipses focus, and I lean into the mountain and fall down. It takes a minute or two for me to get back up. I'm regretting my decision. After two more wipeouts and a number of tense and flawed turns, I make it off the blue terrain and back into easier green territory.

But it doesn't matter. My calm rattled, I somehow lose my right ski as I descend to the flatter topography. A girl nudges it to me as she passes, but I can't seem to get it back on. Doug is nowhere in sight.

I curse as I try to stomp my boot into place. This might well be my bad blind date with skiing. I finally get it back on and continue down the hill, hugging the right side and snowplowing. Every muscle in my body is tense.

Not until the long and wide final straightaway do I manage to muster enough toddleresque Zen to get the old mental chimp back on its unicycle. I finish the last third of the run without eating snow.

At the base, a rare case of snowstorm lightning has closed the lift early. Doug and I decide to get a beer.

"It's good you got one long one like that in," Doug says. "That's what skiing is all about. You're almost there. Just a couple more days and you'll have it down."

Hoping to soothe my aching body, I greedily gulp my beer. I ponder whether I should have ever left the beginner's hill.

"If the lifts were still open," I tell Doug, "I would have tried that run again." I'm pretty sure I'm not lying.

Where to go...

Breckenridge Ski Resort
970-453-5000
breckenridge.snow.com

Lodge & Spa at Breckenridge
112 Overlook Dr., Breckenridge
800-736-1607
www.thelodgeatbreck.com

Schussbaumer Ski Club
www.schussbaumer.com

Copper Mountain Ski Resort
866-841-2481
www.coppercolorado.com

Breckenridge Brewery
600 S. Main St., Breckenridge
970-453-1550

Downstairs at Eric's
111 S. Main St., Breckenridge
970-453-1401

Loveland Ski Area
303-569-3203
www.skiloveland.com

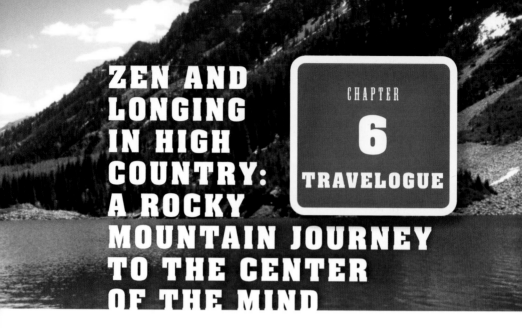

ZEN AND LONGING IN HIGH COUNTRY: A ROCKY MOUNTAIN JOURNEY TO THE CENTER OF THE MIND

II DAYS, 659 MILES

There in the wrap, sunk in the Soft Pak "floating table," I first feel relaxation on the day after the Antichrist was supposed to show, but as usual didn't.

Smothered in goo made of pumpkin and orange and tea leaves, entombed in an expensive German therapy machine, I finally let go of the various snafus that frazzled me earlier in the day in Denver, 2,870 feet below. I have absolutely no reason to be frazzled now (nor earlier, really), because I'm on a cushy writing assignment for an in-flight magazine (reporting on spas, restaurants, and hotels in the Vail Valley) and working an overlapping guide book gig that will take me to Aspen, Steamboat Springs, and beyond. Thus the free pumpkin-goo wrap at the ritzy Aria Spa and accompanying free room at its home resort, Vail Cascade, and many other nibbles on luxury that are far beyond my financial means.

In other words, the perfect backdrop for enlightenment.

Enya-like music plays in my dim therapy room. I feel pretty damn good. Pumpkin and orange smell pretty damn good. I wish I were a baby. I'm sleepy. I'm hot.

I'm really hot. I slowly sway from meditation to discomfort, sweating profusely the whole time.

I want out. I am wrapped like a burrito in pumpkin salsa and a plastic sheet.

Diane, my therapist, returns. "Are you ready to come out?"

"Yes, I think so."

Soon after being freed from my cocoon, Diane gives me an invigorating lotion massage and my mind revisits memories of birth, my mom telling me everything is okay, and adolescent longing. My left buttock tenses when she gives it a good kneading, but I stay otherwise calm. I forget about the pay-as-you-go cell phone crap-out, the ATM strip burnout, the overflowing voicemail.

Oddly enough, I'm mad at myself for getting irritated by my earlier stresses mere minutes after being released from the serenity of the spa. At one point, I wanted to move into that organic body wrap and never leave. But now I'm back out in the nearly independent city-state of the Vail Cascade within the synthetic resort environs of Vail, pissed off for no good reason.

The resort's sales director treats me to dinner. I eat buffalo ribeye and drink wine and forget about everything, and later sit on my balcony and listen to the roar of Gore Creek drown out *The Best of Emmylou Harris*.

· · · · ·

My next day of pampered enlightenment finds me drinking margaritas and gobbling down a quail/enchilada combo at the Minturn Saloon while slumbering at the ridiculously fancy Ritz-Carlton, Bachelor Gulch, near Beaver Creek. A masseuse named Anna gives me the first authentic Swedish massage of my life, and undoubtedly the best.

Why can't I teach myself to attain this level of relaxation on my own?

After rising to yet another day full of interviews and tours, I cap it off with a fantastic wine-paired six-course dinner with the in-flight magazine's photographer at Kelly Liken Restaurant. Buzzed, the hour nearing midnight, I make it back to my penthouse suite at the freshly rebuilt *Shining*-like-empty Tivoli Lodge and look out on the dark mountain, nearly devoid of snow, and the empty town below.

It's my last night in Vail. I'm leaving just as I start to get comfortable.

· · · · ·

Aspen is ridiculous. Glitz and hype and money, a little suburb of Beverly Hills 1,000 miles from the Pacific Ocean. But it's just a short drive from the Maroon Bells, a vast tract of perfect roadless wilderness, and it's only fifteen miles as the crow flies to Crested Butte. To reach Crested Butte via asphalt, however, is 300 miles. Hiking around Maroon Lake, I find it hard to ignore such beauty, and even harder to lose control of my emotions in the face of it.

I finish my spa and restaurant reviews just before deadline and transition to guidebook author, checking out glitzy new restaurants and hotels. My second night in Aspen I take the bus to the Woody Creek Tavern and have some endorphin-inducing tamales and plenty of margaritas and beer. I talk the ear off of Ric Rock, the bartender. He talks back.

"I think this administration is like Nazi fucking Germany," Ric says at one point.

"What was the only show The Beatles didn't sell out on their first U.S. tour?" I ask him later. I had to tell him Red Rocks was the answer.

I take a break from my bar stool and climb the ridge above Woody Creek (which is the tavern and a trailer park surrounded by the holdings of large property owners, surrounded by mountainous wildlands) and smoke some weed. An inactive bulldozer sits on the side of a big hole it apparently had previously dug.

I go back down. Ric knows nothing of the project. I give him a copy of a book I wrote, as a tip. He is quite concerned about me driving.

"I'm not driving anywhere," I slur. "I gotta ride coming."

My ride is Jon Barnes, the owner of the Ultimate Taxi. I smoke more weed. He has a computer monitor on the dash, where he plays a roller coaster simulator that almost makes me puke. Then he puts on a light show, jams out on an odd wind-instrument synthesizer, gives me 3-D glasses, and drops me off at the Limelight Lodge just before my bladder bursts. I show good judgment and go to bed.

· · · · ·

The next morning I tour the chic Sky Hotel, which has about the smallest $500 rooms I've ever seen, and then drive several hours from Aspen to Steamboat Springs. I wander around the mostly deserted ski village and drink beers with locals and second-home owners.

I feel my temper rise on the trail the following afternoon. I am hiking to Strawberry Park Hot Springs, a funky mountain facility that's reachable by car, but I've chosen the back way: three miles through the forest by boot. My aggravation started earlier, some combination of needing to go to the bathroom while in a semi-annoying conversation. Next thing I know, I'm hot and sweaty on the trail and my mood is sour.

It culminates with me cursing nothing in particular after I feel the manager of the hot springs blows me off. I climb the hill and poke around a caboose that's been converted into a kitchenette.

I'm still mad, for no good reason. Must get control. I go into the springs for a soak. My anger melts away in the 100-degree water. The surrounding forest, the babbling creek, the sun…why was I mad? And why do I require a soak or a massage or some other external stimulus to soothe the wrath within?

On the hike out, my mood improves significantly. Cloud cover eases the heat, lizards and butterflies and wildflowers keep me company, and I make it back to my car around 5 p.m.

I bounce around downtown Steamboat Springs that night and run into Jessica, the young bookstore manager I'd met earlier in the day, at Sunpies, a bar on the Yampa River. I have what she's having, a sugary, rummy "Slurricane." I feel out of place with the young, semi-extreme ski-bum bar scene and eventually feel like the old, confused guy while sharing a taxi back to my condo with Jessica and her friends.

The next day I have lunch with Blair, a sales guy for Steamboat Resorts. I tell him of my plans: to spend the night at the Home Ranch, an ultra-luxury guest ranch thirty miles north of town in Clark, then head to State Bridge, a legendary biker and hippie party spot an hour south of Steamboat.

All one

He finds it pretty amusing that I am planning on going from an $800-a-night cabin to a $50-a-night one. In my eyes they are somehow equal, since I am being comped for both.

"This may be the first time someone has stayed at these two particular places on consecutive nights," I hypothesize.

He agrees. "I'm sure of it."

I tell him it also will be fun to go from one extreme to the other. This makes me feel calm:

to feel comfortable anytime, anywhere. To feel out of place is its natural antithesis, an anxious state.

. . . . .

Later at the Home Ranch, I quickly strip down and get into my private outdoor hot tub, accidentally dipping my towel in the tub as I do. "Goddamnit," I say with a snarl that melts into a smile when I realize how ludicrous it is to be angry at the situation. A comp room at a posh guest ranch with a private hot tub outweigh even a fully saturated towel. I feel utterly calm in that tub, especially after locating the switch for the Moto Massage. I close my eyes.

Should I buy a hot tub? I think I need one.

I open my eyes. Aspen trees. Mountain views. A deer ambles by, grazing. Zen.

As I get out of the hot tub, I realize the jets have been obscuring the meows of a cat that is onto the scents of mesquite turkey and brie emanating from my fridge. I shut the closet where the fridge is tucked away, but the cat—bony and animated with a big divot missing from its left ear—is stubborn. It meows and meows and rubs against everything. It seems incredibly hungry, but I'm not going to condition it to claw at my door all night. I begin to think it might be feral, so I shoo it away and shut my cabin door.

In the late afternoon, I ignore the signs of a pending thunderstorm and hike the trails behind the Home Ranch for an hour. I climb up a gently sloping mountainside dominated by a vast aspen grove. It is open range, too, so I come across some grazing cattle and accidentally spook them away. As I steadily hike, gaining a few inches of elevation with every step, it dawns on me. It's all one.

Each and every aspen in the grove is all one. Aspen trees share the same root system, meaning massive stands of aspen are actually just one organism. Along with the Great Barrier Reef and a massive underground fungus in Oregon, the largest stands of aspen in the Rockies are among the biggest single living things on the planet.

It's all one.

A level of calm takes over. My feeling in place equaling calm makes sense, and my searching for external stimuli to dampen emotion produced by external stimuli seems illogical. Peace comes from within.

I look at the aspen as I hike the trail, mentally crafting a metaphor for humanity as the stand, each aspen an individual in society and ultimately connected to everyone else.

I am but one aspen. We are all connected. Some aspens support other aspens that would have otherwise fallen. I feel like an aspen.

It's all one.

I have no idea what the cows represent.

· · · · ·

I get my fancy Rockmount Western shirt and boots from the car for the 6 p.m. margarita hour. When I return to my cabin, the cat emerges from under the porch and meows. He evidently is still hungry. So am I.

Dinner is terrific, a polenta-like bed of grits for scallop and shrimp, drizzled in bourbon sauce. Tiramisu means to lift up, the chef tells us, and that it does. The guests and I later commiserate over our shared disdain for the petroleum economy.

Then it's back to the hot tub. It feels good, but my aspen Zen is gone for the night. It's hard to feel you're part of one big whole when you're alone.

· · · · ·

I regain my inner peace the next morning in the aspen grove. This time I am on horseback (for the first time since I was four) with a wrangler named Greg.

"Aspen are real interesting trees," Greg says as he hops off his horse to clear some wood from the trail. "They don't live very long, and they have an interesting root structure."

"It's all one," I respond. I tell him about my metaphor and ask the career English teacher what the cows might be. He's stumped.

My horse is Hopi. Skittish at first, he warms up to me as the ride goes on. He seems much more interested in eating grass than transporting me, but we work it out in the end. "Relaxed alertness" is what Greg describes as the perfect equestrian mind-set. Knowing when to be gentle and when to be firm also strikes me as critical. Just about anything can immediately rile Hopi up.

After lunch, alone amidst the upper-class vacationing families and the meowing cat fixated on the grill, I leave for State Bridge, listening to Greg's *Cowboy Fandango* and The Shaggs en route.

As I drive through Oak Creek, I think about connectedness and humanity in general. Everything I say, think, and experience is based on previous generations of people and what they saw, thought, and experienced; same goes for everybody else. It's so easy to have hyper-individualistic tunnel vision and forget that we're all one. I also take a picture of a big set of mechanical jaws that hauled coal out of these mountains until 1996, when the Edna coal mine closed.

· · · · ·

State Bridge's reputation precedes it. A favorite of bikers and hippies, it sits next to the Colorado River and the tracks where Amtrak trains and coal trains and rafters and kayakers continually pass. It is right next to the bridge of the same name, and is known for its concerts (mostly jam bands, but the Dixie Chicks played here in 1996) and saloon. Under new ownership, it looks to be on the upswing.

I check into the cabin next to the cabin where Teddy Roosevelt slept when he was briefly vice president in 1901, right before he took over following the untimely demise of William Henry Harrison, whose main claim to fame today is dying. At 4:25 p.m., reasoning that 4:20 p.m. is horrible due to its Hitler/Columbine connotations, I hike to the top of a red volcanic finger for some rest and relaxation. Once down, I shower and head off to Friday happy hour at the Wolcott Yacht Club, a hobnobbing time and place of note for Vail Valley locals. I'd driven right by it on U.S. 6 a week before, and should have stopped then. But Friday happy hour is the place's prime time, and the silicone is out in full force.

The see-and-be-seen crowd at the riverside bar and grill is a marked contrast to the sparse, odd mix of tourists and hippies at the State Bridge bar I'll see later. But I will say that the hippies on the river seem to have something down right, as do the ski bums, fly-fishing guides, whitewater

freaks, et cetera: They know how to take it easy. Too fucking easy sometimes. The bartender in Wolcott tells me he's been in the area for sixteen years and has a condo in Vail. I think he must be a ski bum who bought a gold mine—condos in Vail have skyrocketed from $200,000 to $1.6 million in the last decade—but he is actually just psyched that he is renting one for only $600 a month. And he doesn't even sleep there outside of ski season.

Maybe a little bit of stress and self-flagellation isn't such a bad thing after all. The flip side, of course, is that I only get mad about the most trivial of things, typically fired up by pointlessly volatile dipshit testosterone. Everything is pointless, and nothing is meaningless.

· · · · ·

Gunnar Linne's ancestors were from Norway, just like mine. We're talking at the bar in State Bridge later that night. He's bounced around the West for a decade or so, from the Oregon Coast to the Colorado Rockies and everywhere else via thumb, and he's a big snow sports guy, working sunburned construction in the summer off-season. He tells me my sense of disconnectedness is all in my mind.

Wait. He's right, no? My neuroses are clearly visible. I am the odd aspen in the stand, shared root structure or not.

Why the anger? Why the why-me? Why did my dog have to die?

Later, the train is passing. I go out to watch and mostly listen to it chug and screech by in the dark. Its industrial cacophony is somehow soothing.

Coal train keeps on rollin'

• • • • •

I wake the next morning and get a cup of coffee. It's an incredible summer morning in the Rockies, the Colorado River coursing by, cloudless but still a bit cool. A bird flies in through the open cabin door and briefly hovers above me before heading back outside.

I hike along the old abandoned stage road along the Colorado River. While crossing the new State Bridge (the original is only pilings), a van with "PERCEPTION" spray-painted on its hood passes by. A quarter-mile down the trail, I startle a five-foot-long yellow snake, and vice versa. It stares at me, poised to strike, but the confrontation is avoided. I pick up a small stone in case another serpent is sunbathing on the trail.

I stop at a footbridge, consider the creek and the river and the world's water as another aspenlike connectedness metaphor, then think of Gunnar, who told me he'd hitched 100,000 miles one year and traveled the West extensively, in a far different manner than my typically car-bound M.O., with travel writer's perks.

On the hike back, I prepare for another encounter with the serpent. I ready my rock, imagining it waiting there for me. A train shows up to add noisy tension to the moment as I round the bend where the first run-in occurred. But the snake is nowhere to be found.

I make it back to my cabin without further incident, except for passing a middle-aged guy with a mullet, Oakley sun-glasses, and a tie-dyed Rolling Stones tee.

Serpent!

• • • • •

"Somebody might be sitting there," K. K. tells me as I slide onto a barstool at her empty outdoor bar and grill a stone's throw from the Colorado River. "I don't know if he's particular about his seat." She is joking, but I don't realize just how much personality she has at this early hour in the day.

I decide to move down two stools for good measure and start to learn exactly why K. K.'s BBQ at Rancho Del Rio is indeed the center of the universe. After all, that's what the sign says, in all caps.

K. K. is perhaps the most skilled one-person bar and grill in the history of mankind. With a propane grill, a pina bar, and the help of the occasional regular, she serves up rib after rib after brat after "4K" after "Little Beauty" after "Orgasmatronic Sundae." Help yourself to beers out of the cooler, but be sure to keep track of exactly how many you have.

And K. K. dispenses as much warped wisdom and funny jokes as she does beef and beer.

On complainers: "Go across the street."

I look across the street and see a mountain. "What's across the street?"

"Exactly."

On the cops: "They're getting a little nosy for as far out in the country as we are."

On cowboy foreplay: "Get in the truck, bitch!"

She only allows one napkin per customer, because she doesn't promote waste. Everything is served on wax paper. She sells beer and airline bottles of booze, but no non-alcoholic beverages; get them at the store up the hill. She also likes to ring a bunch of bells.

I have a 4K (short for K. K.'s Klassic Kombination: split Italian sausage atop a cheeseburger with fresh jalapeños) and a couple of Buds, then mosey a hundred yards or so to the Colorado River Center, where I rent an inflatable kayak and paddle four miles down the Colorado to State Bridge, where a shuttle picks me up and takes me back to a barstool at K. K.'s.

On the river, it hits me that it is the perfect day. My aspen/river Zen radiates from deep within. I spin slowly in the slow blue water under the sun, occasionally perking up for a splash of low-key whitewater. Everything is right with the world.

Rancho Del Rio started as a commune in the late 1960s and evolved into what it is today: a community of twenty or so residents in cabins and trailers, several rafting companies and fishing guides, and the Colorado River snaking by under the green-studded red and grey mountainscape. And K. K.'s BBQ.

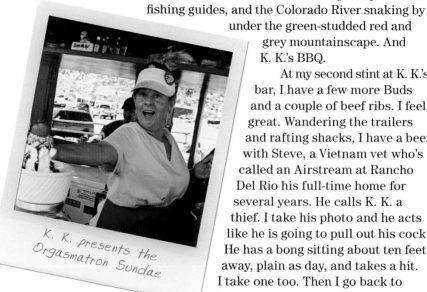

K. K. presents the Orgasmatron Sundae

At my second stint at K. K.'s bar, I have a few more Buds and a couple of beef ribs. I feel great. Wandering the trailers and rafting shacks, I have a beer with Steve, a Vietnam vet who's called an Airstream at Rancho Del Rio his full-time home for several years. He calls K. K. a thief. I take his photo and he acts like he is going to pull out his cock. He has a bong sitting about ten feet away, plain as day, and takes a hit. I take one too. Then I go back to State Bridge.

My seemingly infinite inner peace lasts about five hours. A combination of beer and the inability to socialize with the hippies in attendance leads me to abandon the bluegrass show for my cabin.

All day long, in my pocket I've carried the stone I'd planned on throwing at the snake, from the hike to the river to K. K.'s to bed. As I'm stripping down for bed, I liken the rock to my temper. I can chuck it at something or someone anytime, but it is critical not to—especially if we're all one, and also especially if I want to stay out of jail.

"Sure, you can avoid the snake," I mumble to no one in particular, "but you can also throw a rock at it."

· · · · ·

I wake up a bit frazzled and hungover, without the beer buzz and exhaustion that led to my emotional crash-and-burn the night before. I feel placid, but ready for another change of scenery.

I bid adieu to Scott, the general manager of State Bridge. "Safe travels," he says.

"I don't know where the fuck I'm going," I tell him.

Actually I do know where the fuck I'm going. I take four highways and a semi-paved mountain road 160 miles to the Shambhala Mountain Center near Red Feather Lakes. I am somehow comped a canvas-sided tent cabin, complete with foam-pad mattress. In a week, I've moved from a cushy suite at the Ritz to a tent with pine needles on the dirty wood floor and no electricity. I might be getting somewhere.

I set out up the hill for the Great Stupa of Dharmakaya Which Liberates Upon Seeing, perched high in a mountain valley. I see it and feel moderately liberated. Before making my final approach, I leave the snake rock (my metaphoric bad temper) and my favorite pen, which was running out of ink anyway, in the offering bowl at the base of the staircase that leads up to the stupa. It is meant for people to leave favorite possessions to cast off the shackles of the material world and the relevant suffering. Others had cast off money, a Barbie doll, a small, framed picture of Mister Rogers, even a cell phone.

Then I walk two slow counterclockwise laps around the stupa's base. It is simply mind over matter. I can only control my reactions to situations, not the situations themselves. Inner peace is called "inner" for a reason. I take off my Chuck Taylors and my ball cap and enter the stupa to meditate at the foot of the statue that contains Chogyam Trungpa Rinpoche's skull. I breathe deep and exhale, breathe deep and try to be the breath, breathe deep. Anger only gets in the way. I take another breath.

Not quite enlightenment, maybe, but it feels pretty damn good.

Where to go...

Vail Cascade
1300 Westhaven Dr., Vail
970-476-7111
www.vailcascade.com

Minturn Saloon
146 N. Main St., Minturn
970-827-5954

Ritz-Carlton, Bachelor Gulch
0130 Daybreak Rdg., Avon
970-748-6200
www.ritzcarlton.com

Kelly Liken Restaurant
12 Vail Rd., Ste. 100, Vail
970-479-0175

Tivoli Lodge
386 Hanson Rd., Vail
800-451-4756
www.tivolilodge.com

Maroon Bells
Aspen
www.coloradowilderness.com

Woody Creek Tavern
2858 Woody Creek Rd., Woody Creek
970-923-4585

**The World Famous
Ultimate Taxi**
Aspen
970-927-9239
www.ultimatetaxi.com

Limelight Lodge
355 S. Monarch St., Aspen
800-433-0832
www.limelightlodge.com

Sky Hotel
709 E. Durant Ave., Aspen
800-882-2582
www.theskyhotel.com

Strawberry Park Hot Springs
44200 CR 36, Steamboat Springs
970-879-0342
www.strawberryhotsprings.com

Sunpies Bistro
735 Yampa Ave., Steamboat
Springs
970-870-3360

Home Ranch
54880 CR 129, Clark
970-879-1780
www.homeranch.com

State Bridge Lodge
Sadly closed,
due to a 2007 fire
www.statebridge.com
for current information

Wolcott Yacht Club
27190 Hwy. 6, Wolcott
970-926-3444

K. K.'s BBQ
The Center of the Universe
Rancho Del Rio
4199 Trough Rd., Bond
970-653-4431
www.ranchodelrio.com

Colorado River Center
Edwards
888-888-7238
www.coloradorivercenter.com

Shambhala Mountain Center
4921 CR 68-C, Red Feather Lakes
888-788-7221
www.shambhalamountain.org

SOUTHWESTERN COLORADO

INTRODUCTION

The Anasazi people lived in this region from about 1000 B.C. to A.D. 1200 Near the end of their run, the Anasazi's population tripled, and then it tripled again. Next they pretty much disappeared without a trace—although a few of the rare traces indicate they were quite violent and perhaps even cannibalistic during their flight.

Some say they overextended the food supply as their population peaked before a major drought. Others believe they were absorbed into nearby Navajo and Ute tribes. Still others point to the Anasazi's vanishing act as proof positive that we are destined to repeat history out here in the arid Southwest.

This booming chunk of Colorado has more ties to the mythical Southwest, extending from West Texas to southern California, than it does with the so-called Rocky Mountain West. A boom-and-bust railroad town oozing with 1880s charm, Durango is the centerpiece city, and the population of its home county, La Plata, inflated by about 25 percent in the 1990s. It's easy to see why people move from all over to reinvent themselves in this far-flung corner: It's drool-inducingly beautiful, full of red rocks and green mesas, and has a laid-back vibe that puts even Boulder to shame.

The Southwest motif might trump all comers down here, but there is still plenty in the way of Rocky Mountain recreation: skiing at Telluride and Durango Mountain—the latter the bland rebranding of the formerly wonderfully blasphemous Purgatory—and hiking and biking on the peaks and in the canyons.

STATS & FACTS

- Rugged San Juan County is the only county in the entire United States without any agriculture.

- Thanks to renegade genius Nikola Tesla, Telluride had electricity before any other city in the world, even Paris, the so-called City of Lights.

- Durango is said to have more bars per capita than any other city in Colorado. As of this writing, the unscientific estimate was one bar per 714 people, compared to Denver's one bar per 1,858 people.

- Since the 1970s, Telluride residents have swapped old household goods at the Freebox, a collection of wooden bins on North Pine Street where on any given day you might find a bottle of booze, last season's fashions, or old skis.

And while southwest Colorado remains relatively sparse in terms of population, eco-minded doomsayers point back to the Anasazi and say, "Just wait 'til that next thousand-year drought. Then you'll have no choice but to abandon this little chunk of gnarled wonderland for another tribe." Just cross your fingers cannibalism won't rear its ugly head again if the fast-food restaurants shut down.

BIG THINGS AND OTHER ROAD ART

Bishop Castle
CO 165, west of Beulah
719-485-3040

One of Colorado's most preeminent—and quirkiest—roadside attractions, Bishop Castle is still a work in progress. Jim Bishop started his big, strange castle in 1959 and now dubs it "the largest one-man construction project in the world." No kidding. A colossal castle made from rocks collected out of the surrounding forest, the castle has a 160-foot tower and is watched over by a steel dragon with a flamethrower in its throat. Next, Bishop wants to surround the 2.5-acre property

with a two-story rock wall with an internal walkway, a project that dwarfs the castle in scope. Considering the unfinished state of the castle's interior, and the somewhat scary climb to the top of the towers (great views, but wobbly platforms, wide-open windows, and gusting winds), it might be a long time before the wall is finished. Another hurdle: There is nary a rock left in sight from the tippy top. But Bishop's persistence has surprised just about every castle visitor to date, so don't count him out.

Read:

- Anything by Louis L'Amour (who wrote many of his books at Durango's Strater Hotel, room 222)

Listen:

- If you're around for the summer solstice, any one of the performers at the annual Telluride Bluegrass Festival

Watch:

- Butch Cassidy and the Sundance Kid, National Lampoon's Family Vacation

To-Do Checklist:

- Discover this wondrous place

- Move here

- Move away

Giant Arrows
U.S. 160, just west of Mancos

The best oversized Southwestern kitsch this side of Holbrook, Arizona, these roadside icons serve as advertising for The Hogan Trading Post. The immense projectiles—telephone poles in a former life—have been deemed un–P.C. by citizens of the Ute Mountain Nation. The furor has been minimal, however: One Ute leader said they were "more tacky than insulting."

Four Corners Monument
At the intersection of the Colorado, Utah, New Mexico, and Arizona state lines
www.navajonationparks.org

If four imaginary lines cross each other in a country that doesn't think much of said imaginary lines, are those lines still imaginary? Yes, they are, especially if you can charge $3 to take a closer look at those lines.

A unit of the Navajo Nation Tribal Parks system, the Four Corners Monument is a slab of flagpole-festooned concrete that offers visitors the unique opportunity to cleave their being into four states at once. It pretty much feels the same as existing in only one state at a time, but there's a certain mental satisfaction to being existentially above state lines because of said division.

I'm not sure which state's laws have precedence in case of a crime. In case such an event occurs, I'd recommend a hasty retreat from Utah.

World's Largest Rocking Chair
CO 115, Penrose

Sadly, at the time of this writing, corralled behind a chain-link fence topped with barbwire—as if it were some sort of secret weapon—the World's Largest Rocking Chair may no longer be available for rocking, but until someone tops its twenty-one-foot, 9,100-pound dimensions, it's still a world record. Located at a shuttered eatery, the chair still makes for a good photo op if you stick your camera's lens through the fence.

Cano's El Castillo
Pine St., east of U.S. 285, Antonito

A metallic counterpoint to Bishop Castle near Beulah, Donald "Cano" Espinoza's aluminum- and hubcap-laden multispired residence is a functional piece of folk art he's been constructing since 1980. A memorial to his late mother and a fallen friend, the semi-contradictory messaging adorning "El Castillo" extols Jesus and bad-mouths booze while incorporating countless beer cans into its wondrous post-apocalyptic-meets-recycled-junk design. On my visit, I met a timid but friendly puppy, waved to Espinoza above, and took note of the slogans out front, "Alcohol & Tobacco is Kills, Mary Jane is Healing."

R.I.P.

Snowplow Drivers
Red Mountain Pass
U.S. 550, between Silverton and Ouray

At 11,018 feet above sea level, Red Mountain Pass is one of the highest paved passes in Colorado. It's also one of the snowiest. Three snowplow drivers have lost their lives keeping the treacherously steep, twisty, and avalanche-prone pass open for travel in the winter: Robert Miller in 1970, Terry Kishbaugh in 1978, and Eddie Imel in 1992. When you're passing by on the Million Dollar Highway, stop and thank them and all the other unsung snowplow drivers who keep the Colorado High Country open to lowlanders in the winter.

Old Mose, circa 1870–1904
Grizzly Courtyard, on the campus of Adams State College
First St. and Stadium Ave., Alamosa

After the state "officially" eradicated *Ursus horribilis* in the 1950s, Colorado's last known grizzly bear was killed in the San

Juans in 1979—yet sightings persist. Whether they're out there in the Juans or not, it's hard to forget Old Mose, so named for his perpetual moseying about the mountains surrounding the San Luis Valley. Said to have killed three people and more than 800 head of cattle, Old Mose was a truly giant bear, even by grizzly standards, weighing in at more than 1,100 pounds. Bearing a distinctive paw print thanks to two missing toes on one of his rear feet, Mose's home base was Black Mountain, between Salida and Cañon City, where he was finally vanquished on April 30, 1904, after taking more than 100 bullets. Adopted

as a de facto mascot for the Adams State Grizzlies, the college commemorated Old Mose's thirty-year run on Colorado's most dreaded list in 2006, by dedicating a twelve-foot bronze statue in the aptly named Grizzly Courtyard.

People's Shrine
On the north side of U.S. 160, a few miles west of Walsenburg

This distinctive road-side memorial is a work of collaborative folk art dedicated to anonymous highway fatalities and other nameless loved ones. Its origins are a mystery to me, but the funky People's Shrine is a fitting place for any passerby to pay respects to anyone they miss.

VICE

Last Dollar Saloon
100 E. Colorado Ave., Telluride
970-728-4800
www.lastdollarsaloon.com

Stripped of chichi pretense, the historic dive known as "The Buck" is Telluride's best watering hole. Located in an 1899 brick building that opened as the National Club that year, the bottled beer, loud jukebox, and especially frivolous crowd is as authentic and antitrendy as it gets in this funky-but-glitzy ski town.

Silver Dome Saloon & Music Hall
611 Ohio St., Silver Cliff
719-783-9458

The only geodesic dome bar I've ever drank in, and perhaps the only one on the entire planet, the Silver Dome Saloon is the only watering hole in Silver Cliff. Open since the early 1980s, the intriguing architecture sheaths a friendly blue-collar beer joint with log bars tools and other odd furnishings. On my visit, I had a good talk with a little French bulldog named Amos, took a picture of the crazy bone-monster perched above the bar, and overheard someone say, "I'm a local—don't tell anyone."

Durango Nightlife

For more than a century, Durango has been the epicenter of Four Corners nightlife and all that goes with it. Once a fabled red-light district, downtown Durango still has plenty of places to get your drink on. The historic El Rancho Tavern (975 Main Ave., 970-259-8111, www.elranchotavern.com) and the newer Steamworks Brewery (801 E. Second Ave., 970-259-9200, www.steamworksbrewing.com) are reliably rowdy, and, on the way to the ski resort, so is the Olde Schoolhouse Café and Saloon (46778 U.S. 550, 970-259-2257).

Colorado Prisons
Cañon City and Florence

If your Colorado road trip goes exceedingly bad, your final destination just might be one of the numerous prisons in the Cañon City area. When Colorado became a state in 1876, local leaders had the choice of being the home of University of Colorado or the Colorado State Prison. Since the clink was a more likely stopover for young adults than college at the time, Cañon City took the prison, handing CU to Boulder. While hindsighters criticize the decision, they might be missing the point: The region has emerged as one of the centers of the national maximum-security industry, while CU lately

has only topped national party-school lists. Case in point: The United States Penitentiary Administrative Maximum Facility (a.k.a. Supermax, a.k.a. the Alcatraz of the Rockies), where the roster of past and present inmates includes John Gotti, the Unabomber, the Shoe Bomber, and other infamous rogues, terrorists, mafiosos, neo-Nazis, and gang leaders.

STAR MAPS

Sling Blade, Roger & Me, My Dinner with André, Rushmore, and *Lost in Translation* all premiered at the annual Telluride Film Festival.

Buckskin Joe Frontier Town and Railway near Cañon City served as a location for such classic Western flicks as *Cat Ballou* and *True Grit* and such classic Western flops as *Lightning Jack* and *The Duchess and the Dirtwater Fox*.

Butch Cassidy and the Sundance Kid filmed at a number of locations in and around Durango and Telluride. When Newman and Redford leap from a cliff to escape the closing-in posse, they actually made just a six-foot jump onto a platform above the Las Animas River near Baker's Bridge, edited with footage of stuntmen making a much braver dive into a river in California.

Boxing legend Jack Dempsey was born in Manassa, where there is a bronze statue and a museum dedicated to him.

Road comedy pinnacle *National Lampoon's Family Vacation* was also shot partly in the Durango area: The lobby of the Strater Hotel doubles as that of a Grand Canyon lodge, and the city also doubles as Dodge City, Kansas, in other scenes.

A fourteener in the southern San Juans, Wilson Peak might be better named Mount Coors: The photogenic summit in served as the inspiration for the mountain in the brewery's logo.

HUH?

UFO Watchtower
2.5 miles north of Hooperon on CO 17
719-580-7901
www.ufowatchtower.com

The largest (and oddest) alpine valley on the planet, the San Luis Valley, is rife with legends. Some of the stories claim the valley is an interdimensional nexus frequented by demons and demigods. Others describe buried treasure, sifting sands,

and crystal skulls. Yet others relate unexplained animal deaths—UADs, for short, referring to surgical livestock mutilations in the 1960s and 1970s—and black helicopters supposedly ferrying federal agents engaged in extraterrestrial cover-ups.

Travelers with a special interest in the latter category should make a point of visiting the UFO Watchtower, where about forty sightings have been reported since it opened in 2000. This ordinary metal platform is in the middle of nowhere, free of urban light pollution, and also offers a few bare-bones campsites, a "vortex" called the Healing Garden, and a must-visit gift shop.

Colorado Alligator Farm
Mosca
719-378-2612
www.coloradogators.com

The Young family had been in the fish business, raising their trademark Rocky Mountain tilapia for restaurants and local markets, for a decade when they struck upon an innovative way to get rid of the dead fish that would invariably float in their farm's waters. They bought 100 gators from Florida in 1987 and tossed them into geothermally heated waters that simmered at a steady 87 degrees Fahrenheit.

The Youngs didn't know if the gators would survive the first Rocky Mountain winter, but pretty much all of them did, and as of the twenty-first-century years, the Youngs are in the gator farm business, an unlikely enterprise in the San Luis Valley. The farm is now home to about 400 gators (the Youngs got the breeding down pat after a few years), the largest of which are more than ten feet long and about 500 pounds. In the snow-packed winters, the big reptilians even like to climb up on the snow and soak in the sun's rays. Weather permitting, gator-wrestling classes are available. You can also pose for a picture with the farm's currently most

docile specimen in your hands for a "Certificate of Bravery," personally punched and authenticated by the runt's teeth.

Pagosa Springs Dinosaurs

In 1982, onetime Pagosa Springs resident Myrtle Snow claimed she'd seen dinosaurs several times in the area back in the 1930s, describing them in a letter to *Empire* magazine as "about seven feet tall…grey…a head like a snake, large stout back legs, and a long tail." According to cryptozoologists, who routinely post their sightings on the Internet, there have been increased reports of alleged river dinosaurs in the region in recent years.

Telluride Nothing Festival
www.telluridenothingfestival.com

Held (or, more accurately, not held) in mid-July since 1991, the Telluride Nothing Festival is actually a non-festival. That means there are no tickets necessary, festgoers do nothing, and no activities or events are scheduled.

Blanca Peak: "The Greatest Sanctuary"
Northeast of Alamosa

The fourth-highest mountain in Colorado, 14,345-foot Blanca Peak is the southernmost spire in the Sangre de Cristo Mountains and the centerpiece of what ancient Navajo peoples called "The Greatest Sanctuary." Spread across present-day Colorado, New Mexico, and Arizona, this vast but perfect triangle is home to Blanca Peak—the cradle of humanity, the earth mother—as well as three other extraordinary mountains that define its boundaries: Mount Hesperus (near Durango, the gateway to the underworld), Abalone Mountain (near Flagstaff, Arizona, the gateway to the universe), and

Mount Taylor (near Albuquerque, New Mexico, the center of humanity's government).

Silver Cliff Cemetery

One-half mile south of CO 96 on Mill St., Silver Cliff
www.silvercliffco.com

The historic mining town of Silver Cliff is older than adjoining sister city Westcliffe and outnumbers it about 600 to 500 in terms of population, by even more if you include the luminous flying orbs occasionally seen after dark making hay in the Silver Cliff Cemetery. And if you're in the market for a gravesite, 126-square-foot plots here go for just $100, one of the best real-estate deals in the Rockies.

Hovenweep and Canyon of the Ancients National Monuments

Near the Colorado-Utah border, northwest of Cortez
970-562-4282 and 970-247-4874
www.nps.gov/hove

About a millennia ago, the Anasazi crafted scads of impressive, gravity-defying castles and cliff dwellings, the center of their civilization being Southwestern Colorado and the Four Corners area. They perfected desert agriculture. Then they up and disappeared.

Their handiwork is mostly intact all over the Four Corners region. Mesa Verde National Park (east of Cortez, 970-529-4465, www.nps.gov/meve) attracts the crowds, but Hovenweep and Canyon of the Ancients are barely visited in comparison, two great destinations to glimpse nicely preserved Anasazi villages. Thanks to the arid desert air and their durable sandstone-and-mortar construction, the ruins in Hovenweep and Canyon of the Ancients have held up remarkably well over the course of their 700-plus-year existences. Most experts believe the Anasazi were absorbed into other Southwestern tribes after a great drought incapacitated their agriculture. At least that's what my dad told me, and he says he knows everything.

Trinidad: "Sex Change Capital of the World"

Dr. Stanley Biber started practicing medicine in Trinidad in 1954 and retired in 2003. During the half-century in between, he performed more than 5,000 sex-change operations and earned his town the nickname "Sex Change Capital of the World." His patients included men and women who became women and men, everyone from linebackers and octogenarians, as he earned the reputation as the field's pioneer and best practitioner. The good doctor passed away in 2006, but his practice lives on in the hands of Dr. Marci Bowers, a former sex-change patient herself.

Crestone

Set at the foot of the Sangre de Cristo Mountains, this curious town of less than 100 colorful locals was something of a mining flop, but it's now internationally known for spiritual retreat centers of all flavors: Zen and Tibetan Buddhist, Hindu, Christian, and other religions all have major retreat centers in the vicinity. In fact, spiritual retreats are now the backbone of the local economy. But it's also an artsy, funky place with no drinking laws (residents use the porch of the local liquor store as an outdoor saloon) and a setting as scenic as any town in the West.

GRUB

Telluride Mushroom Festival
Telluride
www.tellurideinstitute.org

'Shroom aficionados unite every August in Telluride to "celebrate and explore all aspects of fungi." Highlighted by a gala dinner where local chefs contribute their best mushroom cuisine, festival speakers include mushroom farmers, mushroom researchers, mushroom photographers, and even the occasional psychonauts.

SLEEPS

Kelloff's Best Western Movie Manor
2830 W. U.S. 160, Monte Vista
800-771-9468
www.bestwestern.com

The only combination drive-in movie theater/motel I know of is located in Monte Vista, and it would be the town's claim to fame except for the fact that there is a major stopover for sandhill cranes in the vicinity. The drive-in dates from 1955; the motel came about a decade later. Speakers in the rooms synch roughly to the movie shown on the screen in the motel's courtyard area. The windows are positioned for a view of the big screen, but alas they also have curtains, which my mom yanked shut here when she felt Cheech and Chong were intruding on our family vacation.

MISC.

Great Sand Dunes National Park and Preserve
Northeast of Alamosa
719-378-6300
www.nps.gov/grsa

Six-foot-six and lanky, Nygard strides up the gargantuan sand hill with surprising ease. At times I feel I am about to lose the battle with gravity with my relatively stubby stems, but I manage to maintain momentum as sand collapses on the side of the enormous dune.

"Are we going up there?" I ask, pointing to the second highest point in sight.

"Nope," replies Nygard. "Up there." As if I had to ask: He points to the absolute highest point, the tippy top of the tallest sand dune in North America, 750 feet from base to peak.

Sweating and cursing under my breath, I trudge up after him. But Nygard is right: Atop High Dune, every ounce of our effort is repaid (and more) by the sweeping views of the thirty-square-mile dunefield and the entire San Luis Valley. We sit and drink water and take it all in, a wondrous geological anomaly that defies expectations.

"When you said sand dunes," says Nygard, "I had no idea they would be this big. This is amazing."

On the way down, we see a kid turn his snowboard into a sandboard, carving his way down 100 feet of silica slope.

THE WESTERN SLOPE

INTRODUCTION

Almost in spite of its mainly abstinent neighbors in Utah, the Western Slope is Colorado's wine country. It's also its peach country, cherry country, and, strangely enough, its fertile mule and headless chicken country.

As the bulge of the Rockies slims down, there are plenty of reasons to veer north or south before hitting the state line. This region, either the state's fertile underbelly or its interestingly sculpted torso, depending on your perspective, is a high desert full of colorful geological wonders crafted by snowmelt, which invariably ends up in the Colorado River. Before picking up steam on its way to the Grand Canyon, the Colorado has plenty of highlights in the state from which it took its name.

Named for the intersection of the Colorado and Gunnison Rivers, Grand Junction is the region's population center and something of a crossroads between Denver, Salt Lake City, and the way to Las Vegas and L.A. The population and economy tend to ebb and flow with energy prices, and lately the boom has been on, thanks to abundant natural gas. And the boom will continue pretty much indefinitely if we get desperate enough to scrape off the irreplaceable surface to get at the huge reserves of oil shale underneath.

All the oil shale below the vineyards means this was once home to a thriving dinosaur population. The fossil bonanza is centered on Dinosaur National Monument on the Utah state line. Between the fossils and the fossil fuels, though, it's clear the latter are more treasured by local industry, and locals spar over conservation versus excavation.

But for now it's for the most part a pristine, sparsely populated slant that is just as devastatingly pretty as Utah, only a Utah that is more into wine and more tolerant of winos.

STATS & FACTS

- The stretch of river from the headwaters in Rocky Mountain National Park to its confluence with the Green in Canyonlands was initially dubbed the Grand, but was renamed in 1921 because state leaders found it awkward that the Colorado River technically started in Utah.

- In the 1970s, archaeologist Jim Jensen made several fossil discoveries near Delta, including some from the largest dinosaur to roam the West, the 130-foot, fifty-ton Supersaurus.

- The plutonium and uranium in the bombs dropped on Hiroshima and Nagasaki were from mines near Grand Junction.

BIG THINGS AND OTHER ROAD ART

Mike the Headless Chicken Statue
Mulberry and Aspen Sts., Fruita
www.miketheheadlesschicken.org

In 1945, Fruita's Lloyd Olsen chopped a rooster's head off but left his brain stem hanging on by a thread. Strangely enough, his behavior didn't change all that much. It follows that  Mike "The Headless Wonder Chicken" toured the country for eighteen months, with Olsen feeding it grain and water with an eyedropper. Mike lived the life of a rock star and was even appraised to be worth $10,000 before dying the death of a rock star: choking in the middle of the night. In 2000, sculptor Lyle Nichols paid testament to Mike's fortitude with a 300-pound semi-abstract sculpture. Fruita also plays host to a festival every May that invites visitors to "Party their heads off" and "Run like a headless chicken" in a 5K.

Rusty's Dream
U.S. 6 and 8th St., in front of Palisades National Bank, Palisade

Dreaming of a world without relief and/or territory marking—which sounds more like a nightmare for most dogs I've known—*Rusty* is the work of sculptor Lyle Nichols, a self-taught local who has plenty of work on adorning street corners in the Grand Valley, including *Mike the Headless Chicken*. In the case of *Rusty's Dream*, mixed-media whiz Nichols made the dog out of rusty bolts and the pedestal, supporting ten cherry-red hydrants, out of granite.

Read:

- High Country News, the great Western publication out of Paonia

Listen:

- Mad Dogs & Englishmen by Joe Cocker, whose home away from the road is Mad Dog Ranch in Crawford

Watch:

- Thelma and Louise, who took part of their fugitive road trip in Unaweep Canyon and Bedrock

To-Do Checklist:

- Pick fruit
- Taste wine
- Sleep in a shady spot
- Repeat

R.I.P.

John Henry "Doc" Holliday, 1851–1887
Old Hill Cemetery, accessible via trail, Glenwood Springs

After earning his D.D.S. from the Pennsylvania College of Dental Surgery, John Henry Holliday went into practice and promptly contracted tuberculosis. Doctors told him he would die within months but that he might extend his life by heading to the drier climates out West. In 1873, he did just that, but his poor health forced him out of dentistry and into gambling, which he was quite good at. His new vocation required he hone his skill in gunfighting, which he also was quite good at.

He hooked up with Wyatt Earp and Bat Masterson and later survived the infamous "Gunfight at the O.K. Corral," gambling, drinking, and coughing his way through the Wild West for much longer than his doctors had predicted. In 1887, after narrowly escaping death by bullet numerous times, Holliday's frail health deteriorated further and he headed to Glenwood Springs to try a new miracle cure: sulfur vapors. They didn't work, and "Doc" lapsed into a two-month coma before awakening, drinking a glass of whiskey, saying, "This is funny," and dying.

Holliday was buried at an indeterminate place in the Old Hill Cemetery, but after his legend grew, the city erected a proper memorial.

Dennis Weaver, 1924–2006

Dennis Weaver Memorial Park
On the Uncompahgre River, north of Ridgway
From U.S. 550, head west at the yellow mailbox

The actor known as the TV cop on *McCloud* and the TV cowboy sidekick on *Gunsmoke* was perhaps more famous later in life for his environmentalism and humanitarianism than his acting resume. Sunridge, his 10,000-square-foot former home outside of Ridgway (on the market for $3.3 million at the time of this writing), is the most celebrated earthship on the planet, made largely with recycled materials—tires, aluminum cans—in its energy-efficient design. Weaver spoke out against our "addiction to fossil fuels," for industrial hemp, and started a number of successful nonprofits to boot.

Weaver is memorialized in his adopted hometown at a sixty-acre park (centered on a 2,800-pound bronze eagle) on a bluff above the Uncompahgre River. The park is a wildlife preserve that is closed November to March in deference to its animal residents.

Chief Ouray, 1833–1880

Ouray Memorial Park at the Ute
Indian Museum
U.S. 550 and Chipeta Dr., 2 miles
south of Montrose

President Rutherford B. Hayes called Ouray "the most intellectual man I've ever conversed with." The hereditary Ute chief rose to power in his teens, and his mastery of languages led him to be a key liaison between the Ute people and Washington, D.C. Chief Ouray pushed for peace, but the westward migration of gold-seekers led

to increased friction in the 1870s. Unfair treatment by the government led to an uprising Ouray could not quell, the infamous Meeker Massacre, which in turn led to the Ute Nation's confinement on a Utah reservation. After the conciliatory peacemaker died young in 1880, he was buried according to Ute custom in a secret mountain grave. But after his wife, Chipeta, passed away forty-four years later, his remains were reinterred beside hers at the Ouray Memorial Park, near Montrose.

VICE

Wolcott Yacht Club
27190 U.S. 6, Wolcott
970-926-3444
www.wolcottyachtclub.com

Granted, Wolcott's yacht inventory is pretty iffy, given its landlocked location and its history as an unincorporated farm town. But the Eagle River runs through town, providing enough water to make for a pretty good joke, which in turn is a pretty good place to have a few beers. The marine-themed bar and grill has one of the best patios in the state, with a great stage and plenty of room to dance, drink, or even withdraw. In the summer, the Friday night outdoor concerts lure imbibers down Vail Pass for the evening (or more), and the riverside location makes for a great booze-and-grub stop for passing rafters and kayakers.

Colorado Wine
www.coloradowine.org

Colorado is generally recognized for its beer, and wine snobs love nothing more than looking down on beer slobs, so Colorado wine gets lost in the fray. While Colorado often out-brews California, Colorado wineries contribute less than one-tenth of 1 percent of the total national wine production; California's output is north of 90 percent.

Grand Valley's grape-growing commenced in the 1880s, but orchards replaced vineyards during Prohibition, and Colorado's viticulture industry didn't take off again until the 1990s. About sixty wineries call the state home today, most of them between Palisade and Grand Junction in the Grand Valley. Dry air, high elevation, and alkaline soils make for grapes that taste more European than Californian. Some say Colorado winemakers are hitting their stride, other critics are less kind, and others still don't really care as long as the samples are free and the wine is alcoholic.

HUH?

Rangely Carrot Men
Moon Canyon, 11.6 miles south of Rangely via CR 23

The Fremont people were active artists in far north-western Colorado a millennia ago, and, their hunched flutist Kokopelli notwithstanding, this might just be their most intriguing work. Tucked away in a rocky chasm south of Rangely, accessible via dirt road and short foot trail, are a number of carrot-shaped, carrot-colored figures, some bearing antennae atop their round heads. Vegetable gods? Carrotlike extraterrestrials who ate humans? Orange ghosts from the future? Your guess is as good as mine.

World's Largest Beaver Dam?
Rifle Falls State Park, Rifle
970-625-1607
www.parks.state.co.us

Legend holds that Rifle Falls is an ancient beaver dam shellacked over the millennia by limestone sediments. Today, the triple waterfall cascades over a cave system that attracts gawkers and spelunkers—but no giant Pleistocene beavers are in sight.

GRUB

Local Produce

The Western Slope is Colorado's fruit basket, with three prime vegetative superstars: Palisade is known for its peaches, Paonia its cherries, and Olathe its sweet corn. (I know corn is not a fruit.) There are orchards and vendors dotting the roadsides all over the area, plus a few annual festivals to boot, namely the Palisade Peach Festival, Paonia Cherry Days, and the Olathe Sweet Corn Festival. (See a pattern yet?) Plus there are plenty of local delicacies made from the bounty, including the legendary fruitcakes and peach cakes baked by the Slice-O-Life Bakery (105 W. Third St., Palisade, 970-464-0577).

MISC.

Colorado National Monument
Southeast of Fruita
970-858-3617
www.nps.gov/colm

Rising above the Grand Valley are the leftovers of millions of years of erosion, a fantasyland of red-rock monoliths, flat mesa, and plunging canyons. Perched on the edge of the vast Colorado Plateau, the monument holds a vast number of nooks and crannies that finders keep as secrets, truly unique spots where one can get lost in the landscape and even temporarily merge with it. Whether it's just the twenty-three-mile scenic drive or an overnight backcountry expedition, any excursion through the Grand Valley should include a detour from I-70 to this remarkably different world above.

Black Canyon of the Gunnison National Park
Northeast of Montrose
970-641-2337
www.nps.gov/blca

A remarkably steep crevice torn from the rock by the Gunnison River, the Black Canyon is much less visited than the Grand Canyon—and much steeper. The Gunnison River drops nearly 100 feet per mile as it shears down the western slope in the park, compared to an average of less than eight feet per mile for the Colorado descending in the Grand. This makes for one of the most dramatic canyons on the planet: At its deepest, the canyon is more than 2,700 feet, at its narrowest, just forty feet.

Measuring 2,250 feet from river to rim, the Painted Wall is the state's highest cliff and one of its best sights at which

to gape and meditate. These improbably steep walls are surprisingly full of life, with pockets of hardy trees and birds
diving into the canyon from all directions, and only a few
hikers a day brave a trip into the canyon itself.

Dinosaur National Monument
East of Dinosaur
970-374-3000
www.nps.gov/dino

While many associate this lesser-known unit of the National
Park Service with the fossil wall across the state line in
Utah, the Colorado side of Dinosaur National Monument is
remote, removed, and remarkable. The monument's eastern
highlight, the jaw-dropping Gates of Lodore—a canyon so
named by the party of famously eccentric explorer John
Wesley Powell—looks like the Green River cut a mountain in
half over the eons. The slow-moving river attracts paddlers
throughout the summer.

TREASURE HUNT

4 DAYS, 1,311 MILES

The morning starts really slow.

    With my buddy Mark—we went to Lewis-Palmer High School together, classes of 1991 (me) and 1994 (Mark)—I'm hunting through the Mt. Pisgah Cemetery in historic Cripple Creek, once a city of 25,000 and the richest mining town in the West. Today the miners are pretty much gone (pop. 1,115), replaced by buses full of septuagenarians to nonagenarians lured by the possibility of a quick buck at the casinos, among the only legal ones in Colorado.

    As a prelude to our road trip looking for legendary lost riches—first Spanish gold in the Sangre de Cristo Mountains, then Butch Cassidy's hidden plunder in the far northwest corner of the state—we're looking for a legendary headstone bearing only the simple inscription "He Called Bill Smith a Liar." After looking for Smith's anonymous victim for a half hour or so, we seek help at the local history museum and learn someone stole the headstone in the 1940s.

    Defeated, we head south out of Cripple Creek on a twisting dirt road through Phantom Canyon, then divert southwest into the Wet Mountain Valley. We talk about how legalized gambling has hurt rather than helped Cripple Creek and how the same goes for the not-so-twin cities of Black Hawk and Central City, west of Denver. In all three of Colorado's gambling towns, greed has trumped historic character and pretty much everything else. The bluehairs are the ones being mined now.

Soon we're driving up a much more rugged dirt road to the trailhead to the legendary Caverna del Oro in the Sangre de Cristos. Mark's behind the wheel of his slick Lexus SUV. My Saturn would not have made it this far.

We're planning to hike up Marble Mountain in search of a cave where Spanish conquistadors allegedly hid a stash of gold 400 years or so ago. Mark spins me the story during our drive: the Spaniards enslaved the indigenous locals to mine gold near the summit, killed them when the mine was picked clean, but ultimately left a big cache of treasure in a cave marked by a cross. Years later—the late 1800s—miners found the cache accompanied by two skeletons, but the cave collapsed before they could recover it.

Thanks to those damn gravestone thieves—who I hope were cursed by their loot—we're running late: It's almost 3 p.m. Sunset is in less than four hours.

Our tennis shoes swapped for hiking boots, we follow the mellow Rainbow Trail to the turnoff, where a sign points us uphill to the Marble Caves. And uphill we trudge. And trudge. And trudge.

On the way, Mark asks me, "Have you ever seen that TV show *I Shouldn't Be Alive*?"

"Never," I reply.

"It's about these people who do something stupid in the wilderness but live to tell about it," he explains. "It's pretty good."

Phantom Canyon tunnel

A couple of miles west and a half-mile skyward later, the evergreen and turning aspen forest is gone, replaced by exposed rock and alpine tundra and the occasional snow-flake. Storm clouds ominously hang atop the mountain and its neighbors in the Sangre de Cristo Range.

We're following directions Mark got from his dad, who grew up in nearby Pueblo, thoroughly exploring these parts. I wander ahead of Mark toward an outcropping of exposed limestone just below the mountain's 13,266-foot summit. It is 5:30 p.m., exactly the time we planned to turn around. Mark is nowhere in sight. I figure he is taking a break somewhere below and start heading downhill to find him, hoping he isn't waiting in ambush, a bar of Spanish gold in one hand and a big rock with my name on it in the other.

Halfway back to timberline, I hear a whistle. Mark has taken a more direct angle toward the outcropping I just retreated from. He yells something unintelligible. I yell an equally unintelligible response and reverse course back uphill.

"Did you find the gold?" I holler once we can actually hear each other.

My partner in crime, Mark

"No, something better," he responds. "A natural spring—water." I make it up to his elevation and he hands me his full Nalgene, cold to the touch. I take a long drink of the best water I've had in a very long time.

But my mental clock is ticking away. "In ten minutes, we should really turn around," I warn. "We don't want to end up on that *I Shouldn't Be Alive* show you were talking about."

Ten minutes later, huffing and puffing at the edge of a crevasse, the sun dropping behind the peak, the storm threatening, we agree we would probably die if we tried to descend this steep and rocky slope in the dark, and we give up on the Spanish gold.

Indeed, we make the last mile of the trip in total darkness. It's scary and sweaty and happily over by about 8 p.m., at which time we make our way to a motel in nearby Westcliffe, followed by a bar and grill for dinner and the Silver Dome Saloon in neighboring Silver Cliff for a nightcap.

Back at our hotel room, Mark nods off while I mindlessly watch the tube. It's been a long day. Just before midnight, he wakes up and heads to the mini-fridge for the remnants of a cheeseburger.

Inside Bishop Castle

"How you doing?" I ask him.

"Pretty good."

"Then let's go back up there and find that cave," I joke.

He laughs at the suggestion. "Then we'd have to drive back out there."

"The drive isn't what I'm worried about."

The next morning we're on the road at 9 a.m. for a full slate of roadside wanderings in the vicinity: Bishop Castle, where a sign reads "Too Bad More & More Everything Is About Money. Please Donate!" We backtrack through Silver Cliff and Westcliffe and zip south through Gardner en route to Walsenburg, where we stop for snacks and gas. I'm in line at the cashier behind a guy who asks for a $10 lottery ticket.

"Which one?" asks the clerk.

"The winning one."

Around 4 p.m. we wander into Crestone, an odd and dinky town right at the foot of the amazing Sangre de Cristos, just over the Continental Divide and 5,000 feet below the peak we

were combing for Spanish gold the evening before. This town is a real looker, with one foot of the Sangres firmly planted downtown. Most roads are dirt, with several deer and one old, happily wagging collie wandering amidst the spiritual retreat centers, ramshackle houses, and adobes.

After wandering around the Baca Grande subdivision in the foothills above and south of town, we decide to stop for a beer at a bar fronted by a busy patio we'd seen in town earlier. But, upon closer inspection, the bar is not a bar, but rather a liquor store; the patio is just several people sitting out front drinking beer. A bit confused but nonetheless thirsty, we walk inside and get ourselves a twelve-pack. There are cockatiels in a cage and complaint forms in the form of a wall-mounted roll of toilet paper.

Out front, we crack a couple of beers and wedge our way into the conversation. I ask about the legends of crystal skulls in the San Luis Valley.

"Aw, no man, that was a fake, a prank," replies a long-haired local known as Jefe. "An artist made it and hid it in a cave near here. Some tourist found it and rumors got out, but it was all fake."

King Mark

"What about Caverna del Oro?" I press.

"What?"

"Have you ever heard of any legends of Spanish gold in the Sangre de Cristos?"

The crowd of approximately five people outside the liquor store comes alive in response. Jefe tells us about miners who found the hidden treasure, cups and helmets and bars all made of gold, and brought two bars each back to town but could never find the cache again when they went back up the mountain.

"Death gold," growls a bearded guy in a trucker hat, lighting a cigarette.

Jefe heads out and Mark and I take our leave soon thereafter, a good ninety-minute drive from our planned refuge for the night, my grandpa's family cabin near South Fork, on the opposite edge of the San Luis Valley.

We get sandwich fixings en route and find the cabin vacant for the night—many a relative holds the key—not surprising with the weather worsening here in early October. After sandwiches, I tell Mark he can have the pullout sofa. I'll take the bed in back.

There's gold in them thar hills

We're having what is agreed upon as one last beer on the porch when headlights appear, followed by a white SUV, its passenger-side window made of duct tape.

We're in the boondocks. It's almost 10 p.m.

"Who the…"

The SUV births a pair of young guys with plenty of piercings and tattoos between them.

"Hey," says one of them. "I'm Helen's grandson Cash."

"I'm Lee's grandson Eric," I introduce myself to my second cousin.

Our respective limbs on the Lamb family tree understood, we shake hands and Cash asks if we'd mind company at the old family cabin for the night.

"No, make yourself at home."

It turns out that it's not just Cash and a cohort, but Cash and three cohorts, all twenty-year-olds from Grand Junction, now living in Durango, studying and partying at Fort Lewis College, heading to the Great Sand Dunes on some sort of consciousness-expanding pilgrimage.

Cash calls yet another cohort on the phone and leaves with one friend in tow to meet him at the highway. Two of the twenty-year-olds and Mark and I, class of 1994 and 1991, respectively (i.e., thirty-one and thirty-four years old, respectively), remain in the cabin. The conversation turns to our meanderings and the legends of Spanish gold hidden in the Sangre de Cristos. I tell the two pierced holdovers the story about the two dudes that found the hoard once but couldn't find it again, and they were incredulous.

"I could never forget something like that hiding place," says the one with the fewer piercings. "That would be the turning point in my life."

"Why would it be the turning point?" I ask.

With that kind of money—i.e., millions of dollars—Mark and I are told, you can invest in mutual funds that will pay many times the investment annually.

"You can do anything you want, at any time," says the more-pierced fellow. "Fly to South America. Go surfing."

Mark and I are fading, and needless to say we share the marginally comfortable queen bed in back and get a sorry night's sleep each. We bid the quintet good luck in their foray into the dunes, and they repeat the gesture. A few minutes later, we're cresting Wolf Creek Pass, leaving the Sangres in the rearview mirror, no gold in hand.

As a guy who runs a plumbing supply business, Mark tells me, "It's amazing how many crooks there are out there." He relates the tale of a guy who wrote a check for $800 for toilets or pipes or whatever and barks to no one in particular on his way out, "I don't have any money in my account," before running away. "The check wasn't dated and I couldn't do shit about it," says Mark.

We descend into Pagosa Springs and continue west to Durango, where we pause for a rest stop at the downtown coffeehouse under Mark's former apartment, a brothel a century or so ago. After passing the multimillion-dollar homes under the banded beauty of Missionary Ridge, we're on the legendary Million Dollar Highway, strung along the mountains between Durango and Silverton and Ouray, up and over several fantastically picturesque mountain passes of the San Juans, past crumbling ruins of mines gone bust and rivers yellow with their residue.

We stop for fast food in Montrose, and Mark tells me another story about some guys with the wholesale wing of his company who kept on adding ones to the front of their paychecks and cashing them at the supermarket, making an extra $1,000 every two weeks with a quick touch-up with a ballpoint pen. Then one day while waiting in line to cash their doctored checks, they foiled an armed robbery and were afterwards hailed as heroes for an entire week—until their forgery ran afoul of the company's accounting.

Pretty soon we've passed the agricultural towns of Olathe and Delta, and Mark is negotiating Grand Junction's Saturday afternoon traffic in search of I-70 west. But we abandon the interstate just before the Utah state line and head west on the much lonelier road to Rangely, in the far northwest corner of the state. Neither of us has been on this road before, and we have been missing out. A mix of ranchland, desert, mountains, and geological anomalies speed by before and after we cross Douglas Pass, a mosaic of fall colors frosted with the first clean and crisp snow of the season.

We divert across a muddy plateau in four-wheel drive before descending to the gravel road to Moon Canyon, the home of the famed Carrot Men pictographs. We struggle to find the right spot. At first the Carrot Men are nowhere in sight, and I race the setting sun along a canyon wall, sweating, jumping vegetation, hopping rocks. Mark goes back to the road above and I plow onward, deeper and deeper into the canyon, until finally I round a corner and the Carrot Men indeed appear. Snapping pictures of the rock art feels as good as finding hidden treasure to me.

I find Mark on the road nearby and I take him back down to the Carrot Men, then we make it to another nearby rock-art site, the Crook Brand site, where we inspect equine inscriptions on a rock wall at dusk.

Mark diverts into a two-foot-wide crack in a formerly intact boulder. "Eric—you better come and check this out."

"What is it?" I ask, scurrying into the crevice toward him.

"I think I found the gold," he says. He's looking down at an army-green artillery box jammed under a few football-sized stones. We uncover the box and find that it's a geocache hidden in this spot by a group who hides boxes of "treasure" in far-flung spots and posts the GPS coordinates of said boxes on the Internet, sending fellow geocachers in search of it.

In this case, the treasure (accompanying a laminated note that explains the above rules of the geocaching game) includes a bunch of souvenir seashells wrapped in plastic, a paperback, chewing gum, and assorted buttons and magnets.

Mark heads back to his car to see what he can leave in the box and returns with a beer cozy, a CD by an obscure Russian band, and a half-tin of Altoids. I take a "Gnomes for Peace" button and pin it on my sweatshirt. Mark doesn't want anything at all.

Twenty minutes later, the sun is down and we're tossing our bags in an $85 room at a motel in Rangely catering to roughnecks in the area's booming energy industry. We take turns in the shower—there is no such luxury at the Lamb family cabin—before heading out to dinner at the Ace High Club and Steak House. We watch the Rockies advance in the playoffs, via satellite, before crashing hard at the motel.

But at 8 a.m. we're again off on our treasure-hunting journey, en route to Brown's Park in the far northwestern corner of the rectangle that is Colorado, where it meets the less precise geometry of Utah and Wyoming. The sage-studded scenery grows increasingly dramatic as we approach the intersection of imaginary lines, the slow waters of the Green River lazily wandering the flat between rugged knobs before knifing into the gaping Gates of Lodore, a dramatic canyon in Dinosaur National Monument.

This is where Butch Cassidy, the Sundance Kid, Tom Horn, and a whole host of other unsavory outlaws took refuge from any or all of the Utah, Wyoming, and Colorado law. Legend has it that Cassidy, born to Mormon parents of Utah before turning to a life of crime by robbing a bank in Telluride in 1889, hid some of his loot in this remote valley. I tell Mark the rumor that Cassidy did not in fact die with Sundance in a hail of Bolivian bullets, but faked his death and snuck back into the U.S. to live to a ripe old age; maybe he swung back here to grab his nest egg. We stop in at the Brown's Park Store (at the same-named campground) for candy, caffeine, and advice.

"I heard Butch Cassidy used to hang out in these parts," I ask the clerk, clearly a longtime local.

"Yep."

"You know where his hidden treasure is buried?"

The brim of the shopkeeper's trucker hat bounces up and down as he laughs. "If I knew that, do you think I'd tell you?"

"Maybe you wouldn't want it. It could be cursed."

"Right."

After I strike a deal to trade any treasure we find for a dusty novelty can of elk assholes in front of the cash register, we press on in the Lexus. After briefly leaving the paved highway to urinate along the side of the gravel road in Utah, we return to Colorado and cross the Green River at Swinging Bridge, where we nervously push the upper end of the bridge's limits of eight feet, five inches in width and three tons in weight. Safely on the west side of the Green's water, ironically tinged red with mud, we find a place to park

where we feel there is a remote possibility of finding Butch
Cassidy's fabled hidden treasure.

But we soon discover that we would need years to
explore this glacier-scored side of Brown's Park, plus years
to explore the other side, and more years yet to discover
the nooks and crannies inside of it. We take a good hike up
into the craggy mountains, following the boundary between
forest fire-scorched and untouched. We see a couple of
possibilities where rocks look too methodically organized
to be the work of Mother Nature, but after pulling up a few
of them by hand—of course we didn't bring a shovel on our
treasure-seeking expedition—we become dubious that the
rocks mark anything at all. The temperature drops notice-
ably as cottony white clouds ooze down the mountain, and
we decide it's best to get going.

"I think it might be easier to work for a living," I tell
Mark, again huffing, puffing, and sweating profusely, "than
hunt for hidden treasure."

On our way out, no gold in hand, we make short meditative stops at an old cemetery, Vermillion Falls, and the
nature trail at the Gates of Lodore. We spook a coyote and
deer as we drive by.

An hour later, we're taking one last stab at hidden treasure: $1 scratch-off lottery tickets at a gas station in Craig. I
get "Bunny Bucks." Mark opts for a "Roulette Riches" and a
quick-pick Powerball ticket for good measure.

We slowly scratch off flakes of latex gold to reveal we
have each won exactly absolutely nothing. My final bounty
from the trip (besides the scratched ticket): a bravery certificate from the alligator farm, the "Gnomes for Peace" button
from the geocache, a caramel-colored rock from Brown's
Park, and a pink rubber ball from a vending machine.

"I've still got my Powerball ticket," says Mark after a
silent moment of remorse for our lost dollars.

"I'm not holding out much hope," I crack, then consider
the possibilities for another silent moment. "But if you win,
will you split it with me?"

Where to go...

Mt. Pisgah Cemetery
Teller County Rd. 1,
just west of downtown
Cripple Creek

**Marble Mountain
Caverna del Oro**
San Isabel National Forest
719-269-8500
www.s.fed.us/r2/psicc

Silver Dome Saloon
611 Ohio St., Silver Cliff
719-783-9458

Bishop Castle
CO 165, west of Beulah
719-485-3040

Million Dollar Highway
San Juan Skyway
www.coloradobyways.org

Moon Canyon
11.6 miles south of Rangely
via CR 23

**Ace High Club and
Steak House**
616 E. Main St., Rangely
970-675-8574

**Dinosaur National
Monument**
Dinosaur
435-781-7700
www.nps.gov/dino

**Browns Park National
Wildlife Refuge**
Northwest of Maybell
via CO 318
970-365-3613
www.fws.gov/brownspark

THE EASTERN PLAINS

INTRODUCTION

When your neighbor is the Rocky Mountains, it's easy to suffer from peak envy.

But residents of Colorado's rural eastern plains, a world away from the Vails and the Tellurides in every way except location, have their own hardscrabble pride.

Many plains folk see Denver as hell on Earth. They know that the real country bumpkins are in Kansas and Nebraska. The air is fresh and clean, except near the feedlots and pigshit lagoons, that is, where it is the exact opposite of fresh and clean. Faith is important, as it is in most places where tornadoes frequent.

But this is also the heart and soul of Colorado agriculture. The state is tops in the production of proso millet (I don't know what that is either) and in the top five in terms of feed cattle, sheep, lettuce, and sunflowers. It follows that a true Colorado dish would be sunflower-crusted lamb on a bed of lettuce and proso millet. (Okay, I looked it up. Proso millet, the only millet grown in the United States, is a grain that's sold primarily as birdseed and health food.)

In recent years, the formerly thriving economy out here has taken a beating as industries evolved and consolidated. As the railroad snaked west in the 1800s, so did many jobs. Refrigerated railcars made it easy to bring Denver fruit from California to Denver, wiping out a considerable amount of agriculture. Today the population continues to trickle west onto the Front Range, which means more boarded-up houses and more piles of abandoned plastic junk.

But not all is lost: The real estate is affordable, alternative energy (most notably wind and ethanol) is booming, and

STATS & FACTS

- Deer Trail claims to be the site of the first rodeo in the United States, held on July 4, 1869. But cowboys in Payson, Arizona, and Pecos, Texas, both claim the title, too. In the end, it depends what definition of *rodeo* you prefer.

- Due to a bad survey in 1867, the imaginary line marking where you leave southeastern Colorado for Kansas and Oklahoma wasn't made official until 1990.

- According to the Colorado Department of Transportation, the southern section of Colorado State Highway 101 in Bent County is the least busy highway in the state, driven by only fifty vehicles daily. In comparison, I-25 near downtown Denver sees about 250,000.

traffic is nonexistent. All things considered, it's much easier to find peace and quiet out on the plains than it is on the peaks of the adjacent Rockies, which attract many more getaways—and are closer to the noisy passing airplanes to boot.

BIG THINGS AND OTHER ROAD ART

Skygrazers
Columbine Park, 3rd St., Sterling

Bradford Rhea (who also carved the staff that President Clinton gave the pope in 1993) whittled a diseased cottonwood tree into this cadre of giraffes stretching their maws toward the clouds. The twenty-foot statue is just one of Rhea's trees-turned-artwork in Sterling, which earned it the nickname "City of Living Trees."

Wonder View Tower
Genoa
719-763-2309

In its heyday, the Wonder View Tower was really something. Built at the highest spot between New York City and the Rockies—nearly 400 feet higher then Denver, at 5,671 feet above sea level—the eighty-foot-tall tower, from the top of which the proprietors claim you can see six states (Colorado, Kansas, Nebraska, Oklahoma, Texas, and New Mexico), was once the anchor of a popular lodging/eatery/dance hall/saloon. Burgers were a dime, and a gallon of wine was a quarter. A stage fronted several dining rooms, where booths were sunk into the funky rock walls, many hand painted with various

Read:

- Centennial by James Michener, Fast Food Nation by Eric Schlosser

Listen:

- Anything by Fort Morgan's favorite son, bandleader Glenn Miller, and a country mixtape (preferably with artists with Colorado ties such as Drag the River, Slim Cessna's Auto Club, and John Denver)

Watch:

- The sunflowers grow

To-Do Checklist:

- Tip a cow
- Race a tractor
- Sit on a porch and do nothing

symbols. "Eat, drink, gas, and pop at the tower" was the slogan back in the day.

Today, it's still something, but we're not quite sure what. Every last room in the place is cluttered with antiques. The paint is peeling. The stairs and ladders up to the tower are shabby. But the view, and a wisp of the roadside mystique, is still intact. As much as things change, some things remain the same.

I don't know if you can really see six states, but there are three two-headed calves in one of the rooms on the main floor.

Junkrassic Park
East of 35 Rd. on JJ Rd., near Cheraw

If you share my bad taste, the colorful gang of characters who call Junkrassic Park home—a group that includes the *Awful Tier* (a junk Eiffel Tower), *El-Vesed Pressed-Lee* (a junk Elvis), and a menagerie of animals—make this worth

the trip out to the middle of nowhere. Despite a vaguely right-wing bent, you can't not enjoy the park's whimsical artwork at this outdoor museum in the middle of miles and miles of farmland.

Madonna of the Plains
Beech and Main Sts., Lamar

One of a dozen such monuments—and the only one in Colorado—this oddly maternal chunk of granite-heavy aggregate naturally honors the mothers who crossed the country on the Santa Fe Trail in covered wagons with their broods.

These statues, erected in the 1920s by the Daughters of the American Revolution, have rifles and babies in their right and left hands, respectively. I include the statue here not because of the rifle, nor the baby, nor the baby-rifle combination, but instead because this rare monument to travelers traversing the plains should be celebrated by all road-trippers, whether they're mothers or not.

Petrified Wood Gas Station
501 N. Main St., Lamar

Now part of a used-car dealership, this intriguing work of rock-art architecture is worth a quick pit stop in Lamar. While in many ways a horrifying waste of a rare natural resource, the structure wins me over with its interesting aesthetics and photogenic nature...but just barely.

R.I.P.

Philip K. Dick, 1928–1982

Outlived by his father, Dick was buried by him alongside his twin sister, Jane C. Dick. The prematurely born pair were separated in death by more than fifty years, as Jane lived only six weeks. Before his time—hell, before our time—Dick wrote mind-bending sci-fi classics like *Do Androids Dream of Electric Sheep?* (which turned into *Blade Runner* on the silver screen) and *The Three Stigmata of Palmer Eldritch*.

Dick mixed drugs, religion, and dysfunction in his pessimistic and surreal near-futures, which are baffling but completely plausible. His final resting place—in a place he never lived, next to a sister he never knew, but always felt—somehow feels appropriate to his off-kilter storyline.

VICE

Julesburg

An eastern journalist once wrote that Julesburg was "the wickedest city in the West." In 1867, Union Pacific deemed the town the "end of track," and the frontier outpost im-

mediately became one of Colorado Territory's biggest towns, teeming with swindlers, prostitutes, bounty hunters, and other Western rogues. Storefronts lining the dusty streets were dominated by saloons, brothels, and gambling dens. Amidst all the drinking and whoremongering, a guy known as "Blacksnake" used to whip cigars out of people's mouths. But soon Cheyenne became UP's new end of track, and most of the wickedness moved on.

So where does modern Julesburg rank on the wickedness scale? Not very high. On my research trip, only one bar was identified, and zero brothels.

Nation's Smallest Jail
211 Main St., Haswell

A perfect counterpoint to Supermax—120 miles to the west—the little town of Haswell advertises its jail as the country's smallest. The 1921 structure measures sixteen feet by fourteen feet, so it could accommodate about two Supermax cells, but the security would be relatively tepid. However, it hasn't housed prisoners since the 1940s, probably because Haswell (pop. 75, probably less by the time you read this) is not exactly a center of criminal activity.

HUH?

Grandpa Jerry's Clown Museum
22 Lincoln Ave., Arriba
719-768-3257

Housing a collection of more than 3,000 clown artifacts, this is most likely the preeminent museum of clown memorabilia in the world. There are paintings of clowns, and figurines, and banks, and music boxes. There are baby rattles and Picasso prints, Ronald McDonald figurines and Jackson Pollockesque Emmet Kelly portraits. There are clowns, lots and lots and lots of clowns.

Jerry Eder started collecting clowns with the help of his brother and lady-friend in 1986 and moved from Sterling to Arriba with his collection in

2001, where it got its own building. Jerry dubs it "the largest collection of its kind in such a small building" but knows of no larger collection in any building.

Jerry says he likes the colors and the smiles and doesn't consider clowns scary—as do many of the *Poltergeist* generation. "I have a lady who collects clowns for me that's scared of them," he says. "She won't even come in here."

Crack Cave
Southwest of Campo

Ogam is an ancient alphabet that traces its roots back to fifth-century Ireland. Strangely enough, researchers have recently identified Ogam petroglyphs on the southeastern Colorado plains, most notably Crack Cave in Picture Canyon. The ornate rock art here is open to the public only by guided tour on the fall equinox, when it shimmers and moves for about ten minutes at dawn. The only other day this happens is the spring equinox.

How ancient Celts got anywhere near here is an even better mystery than Stonehenge's origins. My totally uneducated theory: The ancient druids behind the Ogam inscriptions discovered the secrets of teleportation long ago and managed to teleport from Stonehenge-like rings in Ireland all the way to what is today eastern Colorado. They may have also come up with time travel. In fact, the druids may just be behind pretty much every unexplained mystery on record.

Missile Site Park
10611 Spur 257, Greeley
970-381-7451

Now a county park, this Atlas E site just outside of Greeley once housed a nuclear missile and a crew waiting for the order to annihilate the enemy. Working twenty-four-hour shifts, the crew here patiently waited for World War III from 1960 to

1965, until technological innovation shut Atlas Es down in favor of Atlas Fs, Titans, and Minutemen, superior methods of delivering an unearthly bomb the literal equal of a mountain of dynamite.

In the 1970s, the federal government handed this place over to Weld County, which turned it into Missile Site Park, installing a playground and a few campsites. Given by appointment, tours include a look at the empty clamp that once held a nuclear missile and a display of atomic preparedness memorabilia: sleeves of antique crackers (emergency rations), how-to instructions for building fallout shelters, wax-sheathed medical equipment, drums of drinking water, and the like. On my visit, I was particularly interested in an illustration of a happy family in their eight-by-eight fallout shelter, with little Susie tying her pigtails and smiling while Dad enjoys a relaxing smoke.

GRUB

Rocky Mountain Oysters

Oysters are hard to trust in the isolated Rockies, with their propensity to go bad fast and cause serious distress when they do. It follows that some coast-born migrant must have seen a bull's testicles and decided that they'd do in a pinch.

While the practice of eating wild kingdom genitalia goes back to ancient Rome, Rocky Mountain oysters have their origins in the West of the 1800s, when economical cowpokes tossed them on a hot stove and waited for them to explode like popcorn.

"It's an ethnic food for the area, and it's a novelty," says Linda Tester, co-owner of Kodi's Kafe and Willie Joe's Saloon (217 Main St., Ovid, 970-463-9963), the best place in Colorado to order up a basket of Rocky Mountain oysters and fries. "A lot of people can't get past the thought. If you fool them, they'll eat them, and they'll say, 'That tastes great.'"

Tester says her dad, Willie Joe, used to make them every Saturday at his pool hall, leading her to get into the business years later. Down the street, the Testers' D & L Meats is the 800-pound gorilla of the Rocky Mountain oyster industry, shipping 20,000 pounds of pre-breaded, top-grade bull fry a month. "That's a lot of nuts, isn't it?" deadpans Linda. D & L also sells them raw for about $5 a pound.

MISC.

Low Point in Colorado
East of Wray

Most extreme types like to brag about how many fourteeners they've bagged and their forays to the high point in Colorado, Mount Elbert at 14,433 feet above sea level. Whatever. Blah blah blah.

Personally, I'm more impressed by those who have ventured to the lowest point in Colorado—and the highest low point of any state in the country—where the Arikaree River drains into Kansas, about 3,315 feet above sea level.

Picket Wire Canyonlands
About 25 miles southwest of La Junta
www.fs.fed.us/r2/psicc/coma

Like the Rockies to the West, the Picket Wire Canyonlands are the product of the Purgatoire River. (Early settlers who didn't speak French bastardized *purgatoire* into "picket wire"—it works especially good in your best redneck accent.) This network of interconnected canyons are a serene area where hikers and mountain bikers seldom bump into one another, and the attractions cover both recent history (a century-old graveyard is the final resting place of many Mexican *vaqueros* who ranched the area) and ancient (a limestone bed alongside the Purgatoire contains the country's largest dinosaur track-site, with the astonishingly clear tootsie-prints of bronto-sauruses galore and many of their long-extinct brethren).

Distortions Unlimited
Greeley
www.distortionsonline.com

In the haunted-house industry, Greeley-based Distortions Unlimited is a heavyweight. In business since owner Ed Edmunds sold his motorcycle in 1978 to get a barrel of latex to make masks, the company made its mark with terrifying animatronics, like a doomed prisoner in an electric chair and zombies fighting over a corpse. Distortions has also created inflatable haunted houses in the shape of clown heads and dragons, props for Hollywood movies, and all sorts of other gear for Halloween. Its home county of Weld is an especially fertile test market for their creations, so don't be surprised to see an inflatable giant lying prone in a cornfield or an extravagantly evil haunted house in the area come October.

PLAINS JOURNEY

3 DAYS, 1,330 MILES

I break free of Denver's tangled rush-hour traffic and head northeast. It's an escape route rarely taken on road trips from Denver, U.S. 85 north to Greeley and beyond.

I, for one, usually head west on I-70, toward Colorado's famed ski resorts, Utah's maelstrom of red rock, and the Pacific Ocean. Sometimes I head north or south on I-25, with a final destination of, say, Yellowstone or Tucson.

But northeast to Greeley, then north to Ault, and east again on a road I've never been on before, this is a region whose surface I haven't even scratched. People rarely vacation on Colorado's plains, probably because it's flat and largely empty. The rural economy has been flailing as the population wanes. Back in Denver, people would rather not think about the emerging rural ghetto to the east as they head west to the ski slopes.

Heading on a three-day loop around the vast pastures of eastern Colorado will be totally new territory for me. It's like a whole different country, right in my backyard.

My bladder overflowing with coffee and my sense of direction faltering, I stop at the Pawnee Grassland office on the outskirts of Greeley. I take care of the bladder issue and get directions to the Pawnee Buttes. I mistakenly think these distinctive sandstone buttes are closer to Greeley, but it turns out they are actually over an hour's drive northeast.

I suddenly realize I forgot to confirm my reservation at the Burge Hotel in Holyoke, a lodging that hooked me when I caught wind of its fireplace, impregnated with, among other things, a Civil War cannonball and a mastodon's tooth. I told the owner Carolyn I'd call and confirm by 1 p.m. Nearing 11 a.m., with few communities on the map between me and the Pawnee Buttes, I swing into a gas station in the town of Ault, where I need to turn east, to use a pay phone. (Yes, I have no cell phone.)

The Burge's number is busy. I try again. Still busy. And again. Still busy. Hmmm.

I look at the map. Briggsdale is the only town between me and the Pawnee Buttes. I'll call her from there.

My route is briefly delayed by a truck hauling what appears to be some sort of 100-foot tower, but I make it there and see a gas station with a phone sign on my left. As I signal, I notice the station is closed and the phone ripped from its onetime carapace.

Shit. Carolyn said she would sell out and there were few rooms for rent in the northeastern corner.

I drive south of the highway into Briggsdale proper, a dinky town with a mix of occupied and dilapidated houses, a long vacant redbrick with, in fading paint, "Briggsdale Motor Co.," and very little in the way of hustle and bustle, or even a downtown. I see just one subtly signed market, which doesn't look to be open but displays a sign indicating it is. Parking and sheepishly pushing the door open, I'm met by an elderly woman behind the cash register.

"Do you have a pay phone? I need to confirm my hotel room."

"No, I'm sorry. I don't have a pay phone."

"Do you have any phone? I'll pay you if I can make a call to Holyoke. I'll give you a dollar."

"Okay, you can try." She retrieves a cordless handset from the back room and hands it to me, but for some reason she doesn't seem too confident. "I don't know if it will work."

It takes forever to start ringing, but it eventually does, and Carolyn answers and confirms my room.

Handing back her phone, I thank the woman, buy a package of Reese's Peanut

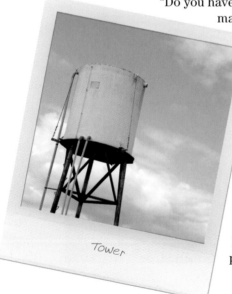

Tower

Butter Cups, and drive away from the eerily quiet little town, a whole different country indeed.

· · · · ·

At noon, after thirty miles on gravel roads crisscrossing the placid sea of boundless grassland, I come over a hill and the view literally takes my breath away. After the homogeneity of the plains, the distinctive hulks of limestone known as the Pawnee Buttes, surrounded by craggy badlands, are surprisingly breathtaking.

Now the landscape is overwhelming around every bend in the road. One almost becomes numb to the everchanging beauty, one jaw-dropping panorama after another. But this sight, set against the subtle landscape of the plains, is pure magic.

Lured to get as close as possible, I hike around the Pawnee Buttes, scrambling along their pedestals in the heat and sun, and make it back to my car at about 1:30 p.m. for the drive to Holyoke.

I have a few stops, of course: Philip K. Dick's grave in Fort Morgan, Skygrazers in Sterling, and Kodi's Kafe in Ovid for some Rocky Mountain oysters.

Speaking with Kodi's proprietors, one tells me, "People don't usually even consider us Colorado. Western Nebraska, maybe."

The other owner mentions that the population has dipped to 400, from a peak of 500. The big sugar plant closed in 1984. "Now we have some empty houses," she says.

I tell her of my loop around Denver to northeastern Colorado, then south to the southeastern corner, then back home.

"I've never been down there," comes the reply. I guess southeastern Colorado is a whole different country for the both of us. And I thought of the plains as vast and more or less united.

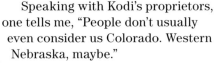

No sugar tonight...

As I finish my testicles, I ask the folks there about must-see stops in northeastern Colorado. I hear about the Julesburg Dragstrip, the second-oldest operating NHRA dragstrip in the country. A picture on the wall of a horse with no hooves on the ground is pointed out. "I can't think of anything else."

I smile and decide it's time to move on. On my way east, the setting sun shines on a graveyard of rusting farm implements, the majestically bleak boarded-up sugar factory next door.

· · · · ·

An hour later, I'm looking at the fireplace in the Burge Hotel, complete with a plaque dated 1929, and the Civil War cannonball, and the mastodon tooth. Phillip, Carolyn's husband, shows me another unique feature amidst the jumble of rocks and stones: a German army helmet from World War I jutting out of the side.

As Phillip shows me to my room, I ask him what there is to do in Holyoke. He smiles. "Go to the bar, I guess. Have dinner. That's about it."

I'd already had deep-fried bull balls for dinner.

· · · · ·

I find the bar a little later, a dinky, woodsy place called Kardale's. Except for the empty stool I take, the bar is full of guys, most in cowboy hats and gimme caps, excitedly talking about the sky-high price of wheat. "If you can't make it this year," says one, looking more golfer or hippie than cowboy, "you might as well bury your head in the sand."

"Six candidates seek five school board positions" reads one front-page story in the local paper lying on the bar. In the classifieds, the cheapest house for sale is $32,000.

I order a second beer. "Where's home for you, sir?" asks the beer-bellied, grey-mustached bartender as he uncaps my bottle.

"Denver."

"I'm sorry."

"Why?"

He doesn't reply before moving on to a more agricultural conversation with the two remaining locals.

· · · · ·

On my way back to the Burge, I notice the train is crossing, as it was an hour before when I'd left the place. I see Phillip before retiring to my room.

"The train," I ask, "does it go all night?"

"Well, you get trains full of grain and trains full of coal going through."

"Trains of coal going east and grain going west?"

"Yep. Tonight's a big night for grain. They'll be moving 'em around for an hour or so."

· · · · ·

After a sporadic night's sleep, I take a bath in the morning. (My $40 room at the Burge has both a kitchen and an in-room jetted tub, but no shower.) Then coffee beckons, so I go downstairs and fill up a Styrofoam cup. I run into Phillip and Carolyn.

"So the hotel," I ask Phillip, "it was built in 1929?"

"What?"

"This place, it's from 1929?"

"Umm…" He clearly doesn't understand what I am saying.

"Was the hotel built in 1929?" I point to the plaque on the fireplace.

"No, that used to be a doorway. The hotel was built in 1887."

He explains that the plaque lists the dozens of traveling salesmen who contributed the rocks and stones—not to mention the cannonball, mastodon tooth, and helmet.

"Who's the most famous person who ever stayed here?" I press on.

"Depends on who you consider famous."

"I don't know—maybe if I've heard of them?"

"I'm sure somebody famous probably stayed here at one time or another."

The conversation ends, and I take my coffee back to my room and prepare for liftoff.

· · · · ·

From the green lawns of Holyoke, I drive south, over undulating bluffs and broad plains, through Wray and Idalia, and a few other small towns. I roll into Arriba around 11:00 a.m. and locate my destination: Grandpa Jerry's Clown Museum.

I'm poking around in the plethora of clowns when Jerry pops up and greets me. He tells me he came back to his home-town of Arriba after forty years in Sterling.

After the grand tour through the three aisles of

How many is too many clowns?

clowns of all kinds, we talk about Arriba. I ask if the population has changed since he originally left.

"It's about half," he says, noting that Arriba had about 400 residents when he graduated high school in the 1950s. "I got three friends who just left. But I kind of like being back in a small town."

Then I drive a few miles west on I-70—which runs right through Denver—to the Wonder View Tower. I'm only ninety-five miles from home when I park my car at this decaying roadside attraction.

I poke into the front room. There is no one there, just tables and displays of dusty antiques for sale. I see a sign that asks patrons to wait at the counter before proceeding to the tower. I follow the sound of a woman's voice down the next hall, and it leads me to a screen door separating the tower and store from the proprietor's living quarters.

A man in a ball cap sits at a dining table. "Hello?" I call out. "Hi, hello. Uh, hello."

He does not respond, so I proceed, following several signs that say "To Tower," through several rooms filled with antiques (primarily dusty bottles, it would seem), and up several increasingly ramshackle staircases, through more rooms with odd relics for sale, and up a couple of rickety ladders to the observation deck, where the owners claim you can see six states. I'm not sure if I can or not, but it is a great view of the plains, the interstate, and the tower complex itself.

In this case, two heads were not better than one

I return down the ladders and check out a room on the ground floor labeled "Grandpa and Grandma's Room." Inside, crickets chirp. Bones and skulls abound, on the walls and

on several display cases. Other antiques are scattered every-where, as before, but I also come across a few two-headed calves and jars once filled with formaldehyde now occupied by desiccated eight-legged pigs and the like. An antique freak show most people would just throw away.

Scared to the front room, admission costs $1 and the man in the ball cap—owner Jerry Chubbuck—is manning it. I explain my entry and pay up, and he points out more rooms to explore, which I do.

It seems before the place became a dusty antique emporium, it was a roadhouse with bands and booze and food, surely a Prohibition hot spot, with cool jumbled-rock construction covered with paintings of all descriptions. Not anymore. Jerry tells me it was "pretty well" shut down when he traded his house and some undisclosed considerations for the tower in the late 1960s.

After Jerry gives me a chance to identify assorted artifacts (such as a walrus penis bone, a chicken-killing tool, and an antique lice comb, among other things), I bid him farewell and drive south to Ordway. Lunch consists of nectarines, potato chips, and Fig Newtons bought at the market in downtown Ordway and eaten in the adjacent park. Then I check in at the adjacent Hotel Ordway, historic but nicely redone for the twenty-first century.

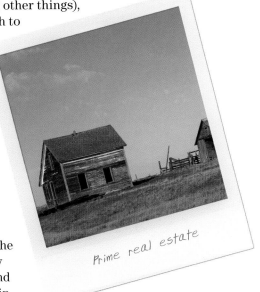

Prime real estate

Next I make my way south to hike in Vogel Canyon, a desolate spot an hour's drive south of Ordway, getting a bit lost on a gravel back road before finding the right road through the seemingly endless prairie, all sunflowers and cactus and tall grasses swaying in the breeze.

Some 500-year-old Indian rock art in the canyon had been defaced over and over, probably first in the 1870s by pioneers on the Santa Fe Trail and most recently by a guy named Frank. In a different area, someone had painted the word *Israel* above a candelabrum. Layer after layer of human history, but at the moment I'm the only human in the entire canyon, perhaps the only one for twenty miles in any direction. Not a soul in sound or sight.

I drive the improbably gorgeous back roads north of La Junta just before sunset, visiting Junkrassic Park before knifing back west through the farmland to Ordway. I drive straight into the fiery sunset and settle into my room just after 7 p.m.

Later I go out for dinner and a beer at the Columbine Saloon, which turns out to be about a century old and spectacularly well preserved, with an ornate back bar and pressed tin ceiling. The bartendress, a tattooed twenty-something with a lip ring, blasts hip-hop, fills my mug with Coors, changes the CD and blasts Journey, refills my mug, and finally tells me she doesn't know the history of the bar.

Like Vogel Canyon, I'm the only one there, at least until some other guy shows up. Wearing sunglasses and a golfer's cap, he says he wants to go crazy and keeps calling people on his cell phone to try and get them to pick him up in Ordway.

Time to call it a day.

I get an early start on my final day of wandering the plains, a good thing because I've got a serious agenda. After stopping at the Sand Creek Massacre National Historic Site, I'm going to drive 100 miles to Holly, a town near the Kansas border that was devastated by a tornado, then drive about another 100 miles to hike Picture Canyon before looping northwest to Denver and my own bed. Can't dillydally too much or I'll be driving until midnight.

En route to stop one, a hand-painted roadside sign begs for a stop: "Nation's Smallest Jail." I drive the wrong way

in Haswell—which is all of a dozen square blocks, give or take—and stop at the city park. Nearby, a couple of Spandex-clad road bikers are readying to embark on some sort of tandem contraption. Afterwards, when I revisit the roadside sign on foot and realize it is a block and a half the other way, a grey cat wanders up to me and acts passive-aggressive as I give it a quick pat. It seems as if it might jump in my car as I rebuckle my seat belt, then stalks my car as I delicately back up and pull around the block.

Having left the anxious feline in the rearview mirror, I photograph the nation's smallest jail and move on. There's a national news story on NPR about the army's wish to expand their Piñon Canyon Maneuver Site—just south of where I hiked the afternoon before—by more than 600 square miles, and the local ranching community's opposition to such a plan. As someone who likes to explore the back roads and trails in the area, I side with the ranchers. I'd hate to see tanks running roughshod over the canyons and ruins of cliff dwellings.

· · · · ·

A half hour later, on a bluff above Big Sandy Creek, the silence is deafening. On November 29, 1864—on the heels of a number of clashes between natives and white settlers—a ragtag group of Union soldiers came here and opened fire on a group of Cheyenne and Arapaho, murdering men, women, and children in cold blood. Before the gruesome facts of the brutal ambush seeped into the public eye, the soldiers were hailed as heroes in Denver. Whistle-blowers were not treated kindly: After one Captain Sailas Soule delivered testimony on what really happened, he was whacked on the streets of Denver. Other witnesses, fearing for their lives, split town. But it didn't take long for the facts of the case to come out, and the tragedy quickly became known as the Sand Creek Massacre.

The bloody scene along the creek is an unseen ghost, today in the guise of a gentle breeze whispering through the leaves and wildflowers. Trailside interpretive signs detail the site's tragic history. "Many of its causes and consequences are as relevant today as they were in 1864" reads one, a sickeningly true statement. We are so bad at learning from our mistakes.

The story has repeated itself over and over and over again, and since long before the states reunited a year after Sand Creek: Public opinion, inflamed by mindless racism and hate, catalyzes an attack on another culture; once cooler heads prevail, horrible crimes (which the public may well have initially interpreted as acts of heroism) come to light. Romans killing Christians, the Crusades, Sand Creek, My Lai, Haditha…

At Sand Creek, sunlight punctures the clouds and momentarily illuminates the landscape. Moments later, the sun again shrouded, I take a deep breath and start back down the bluff to my car.

· · · · ·

Sand Creek Massacre site

Out here on the plains, some of the layers of history are invisible, some are flaking paint, and some are shiny and plastic and selling high-fat fast food. The last of the three, a hallmark of the modern layer, attracts far more people than ancient spots like Vogel Canyon and the Pawnee Buttes.

The sun is shining and I have Wilco playing on the Saturn's stereo. The windows are down. The road is empty from horizon to horizon as the plains wrinkle into hills clad in sunflowers and cacti on either side of the nicely treed Arkansas River.

I'm on my way to Holly. In April 2007—without warning—a tornado with winds of 199 miles per hour ripped through the town of 1,000 residents, destroying thirty-five homes as it tore a two-mile-long gash in the earth, three city-blocks wide. I'm expecting to see devastation, but the scene is much tidier and busier than expected. Rebuilding looks to be in full swing. There are no piles of debris, only numerous once-glass windows still paned with plywood.

Soon I'm driving south on the final north-south route before Colorado becomes Kansas, a remarkably desolate road, even for the plains. It is one of the most back of back roads I've ever driven.

This area around Springfield in far southeastern Colorado was devastated by the Dust Bowl. In the 1930s, drought-ravaged, overfarmed land blew away with the wind and returned to the earth in grand fashion as apocalyptic dust storms—also known as "black blizzards"—that instantly turned the prairie here into sandblasted desert, burying everything in literally inches of dust. These phenomena represent another invisible layer of history, albeit one that many scientists predict will soon replay, not unlike so many reoccurring patterns over the millennia of human domination of the planet.

Soon I turn off on Road N in Campo, eighteen miles of country gravel just north of the Oklahoma state line and the route to Picture Canyon. I see one or two other cars before I park at the trailhead.

Once again, the parking lot is empty. And once again, the rock walls are battle-scarred with etchings, by Angie G. and the Kregers alongside that of the Anasazi.

But here something even more unusual was found adorning some of the rocks: pre-Anasazi petroglyphs researchers recently inexplicably identified as Ogam, an ancient Celtic language.

The buzz of the grasshoppers, the murmur of the wind, the chirping of the birds, and me. Picture Canyon is a great place for a hike. I wish I had more time to explore it, but I need to get back to Denver for band practice.

Stopping several times for photos on the 250-mile drive back home, I feel a sense of inner calm. After my two previous road trips took me to Yellowstone and Newport Beach at peak season, it was quite nice to get away from any semblance of hustle and bustle. I had three great trail systems, all through amazingly picturesque spots, all to myself. Solitude like that is remarkably hard to find on Colorado's mountain trails.

But on the plains, the trails are virtually forgotten, rarely a soul in sight, and just the spot to really and truly get away from it all. As I close in on Denver, the traffic thickens by the mile.

Driving west into an impossibly beautiful ruby-tinted sunset, I surprise myself by wishing I had more time to explore the uncharted territory (for me, that is) out on the plains.

Where to go...

Pawnee National Grassland
25 miles northeast of Greeley
970-295-6600
www.fs.fed.us

Burge Hotel
230 N. Interocean Ave., Holyoke
970-854-2261

Kardale's
142 N. Interocean Ave., Holyoke
970-854-3455

**Grandpa Jerry's
Clown Museum**
22 Lincoln Ave., Arriba
719-768-3257

Wonder View Tower
Genoa
719-763-2309

Hotel Ordway
132 Colorado Ave., Ordway
719-267-3541
www.hotelordway.com

Vogel Canyon
USDA Forest Service
719-384-2181
www.santafetrailscenic
andhistoricbyway.org

Junkrassic Park
East of 35 Rd. on JJ Rd.
Near Cheraw

Columbine Saloon
217 Main St., Ordway
719-267-9990

Nation's Smallest Jail
211 Main St., Haswell

**Sand Creek Massacre
National Historic Site**
Near Eads
719-438-5916, 719-383-5051,
or 719-729-3003
www.nps.gov/sand

Picture Canyon
USDA Forest Service
719-523-6591
www.santafetrail
scenicandhistoricbyway.org

Travel Host
COAST TO COAST
SCENIC HI-WAY

INTERSTATE 70

US 40

US 24

WEST HAVEN MOTEL & RESTAURANT

TRAVEL HOST by V.H. Bushnell
Box 1   Phone: (608) 326-8080
Prairie du Chien, Wisconsin 53821
September, 1977

KANSAS CITY

69

TOPEKA

84

IRA PRICE CAFE

JUNCTION CITY

20

WAGON WHEEL CAFE

Midland Hotel   Wilson, Kan.

70

ABILENE

51

6

156

RUSSELL SALE BARN CAFE

MONTE CARLO MOTEL

13

7   12

ELLSWORTH

Alt. 40   RUSSELL

14

MC ATEE'S "45" RESTAURANT

BOEVE'S COINS & ANTIQUES

5

66

MOM'S PLACE

2   17

2

MIDLAND HOTEL & CAFE

WILSON

18

39

WA KEENEY

ELLIS

Meramac Caverns
Stanton, Mo.

SITES MUSEUM COIN-ANTIQUE SHOP

LITTLE CAFE

PRAIRIE DOG TOWN & GIFT SHOP

Gen. Dwight D.
Eisenhower
Abilene, Kan.

DEEP ROCK CAFE

6

2

BUS DEPOT

FICK FOSSIL MUSEUM

KANSAS

5

COLBY

2

OAKLEY

Prairie Dog
Town

Oakley,
Kansas

BURLINGTON LIQUORS

SLOAN'S MOTEL

I-70 SKELLY SERVICE & CAFE

78

BURLINGTON

Boating & Fishing on Bonny
COLORADO   Dam
near Burlington, Colo

Watch for Exit No. 102
World's Wonder View Tower
near Genoa, Colo.
Follow Points of Interest Signs

54

ARRIBA

Fick Fossil Museum
Oakley, Kan.

GATEWAY to the ROCKIES

HUSKY CAFE

FRONTIER MOTEL

HUSKY SERVICE

SHULL'S PIANOS & ANTIQUES -
TARADO MUSEUM -
SOUVENIR GIFT SHOP -
PACKAGE LIQUOR STORE

12

Gateway to the Rockies
Limon, Colo

GENOA

Exit

State 109

Sites Museum
Coin-Antique Shop
4 Miles N. of
Oakley, Kansas

WORLD'S WONDER VIEW TOWER

9

Boyhood Home of Walter
Chrysler A step into yesteryear
of the 1880's. "No Admission."
Open May 1st to Sept. 1st.
Hours 9 a.m. to 12 noon - 1 p.m. to 5 p.m.

Overpass

WEST LIMON MOTEL

JB STEAK HOUSE & LOUNGE

LIMON

Shull's Pianos and Antiques -
Tarado Museum, Souvenir Gift
Shop, Package Liquor Store,
Arriba, Colo.

89

One of the Largest
Oil Fields in
Kansas

DENVER   Near Russell, Kansas

A Must to see while in Ellis, Kansas

WEST HAVEN MOTEL & RESTAURANT, Kansas City, Kan. 1½ Mi. W. on 24-73 Bus. Rt. 40. Rest. open 6 a.m. to 1:30 a.m. A.C. Serving meals at all hrs. A complete menu. Motel 21 ultra modern units, TV, phones, hot water heat, swimming pool. AAA. ph: 913-287-5250.

IRA PRICE CAFE, Topeka, Kan. On U.S. 24, ½ Mi. E. of Cloverleaf, 3 Mi. E. of new Hwy. 75. Open 24 hrs. daily except Sat. Closed at 9 p.m. till 7 a.m. Sun. A.C. Serving meals at all hrs. Breakfast served any hr. Chicken & steaks a specialty. If you don't see what you want ask for it. "I don't want a million $$, but I do want a million friends." Plenty of parking space.

WAGON WHEEL CAFE, downtown Abilene, Kansas on 206 N. Cedar. Open 6 a.m. to 9 p.m. closed on Mon. Serving a varied menu of quality food very reasonably priced. Fancy U.S. choice steaks & Chops from our own meat market. Fresh seafood & Fish, quick deep fry & grilled items. Soups ready to serve. Homemade pies, rolls & Cinnamon Rolls, "We boast one of the largest menus in this part of Kansas." "If We are Busy - "You'll Be Glad You Waited." Ph: 263-3482.

MC ATEES "45" RESTAURANT, Ellsworth, Kan. Located on Hiways 156-40-14. A.C. Open 6 a.m. to 8 p.m. Mon. Thru. Sat. 7 a.m. to 2:30 p.m. Sun. Serving B.L.D. Good food, quick Service. Huff Fina, Phillips 66 Station, Greyhound Depot, Garden Motel adj.

MIDLAND HOTEL & CAFE, Wilson, Kan. 2 Mi. S. of I-70 on Hwy. 232. Czech & American foods. Czech food by reservation only. Comfortable modern rooms in turn of century atmosphere. Just 8 Mi. N. to beautiful Lake Wilson. Let Agnes Hill be your Hostess in the Czech capital of Kansas.

RUSSELL SALE BARN CAFE, Russell, Kan. Turn off 281 Exit N. to Russell Livestock Commission Co. Bldg. Comp. menu of homecooked food, pies, from our own ovens, homemade soup. Luncheon special daily.

MOM'S PLACE, WaKeeney, Kans. Take I-70 Bux. Loop to Main St. caution light, then N. 2½ blks. W. side of street. A well established restaurant serving a varied menu of homecooked food, pies & rolls fresh daily from our own ovens. Open 6:30 a.m. Mon. thru Sat. Luncheon special daily. Your hostess, Doris Wagg, (Mom).

BOEVE'S COINS & ANTIQUES, located at the Staatz Hotel, downtown WaKeeney, Kans. We carry a general line of antiques, furniture, clocks, glassware, collectables of all kinds. The rooms open 24 hrs. a day, rooms available for rent, reasonable rates, $6.00 and up. John Boeve, Owner & Operator.

LITTLE CAFE, Oakley, Kan. Little Cafe of fine steaks. Smorgasbord each day-noon and night. Phone: 672-4223. Visit Fick Fossil Museum.

SITES MUSEUM, COIN-ANTIQUE SHOP. Oakley, Kansas. Featuring Farm Related Items, including Cast Iron Implement Seats, Agricultural artifacts, hand pounded copper weather vanes and many other items. Jct. Hwy 83 & I-70.Camp Inn - Oakley, Kansas. Hrs. 2-10 p.m. or appointment. Phone 913-672-3324.

PRAIRIE DOG TOWN & GIFT SHOP, Oakley, Kan. Jct. of I-70 & Hwy. 83. Inflation? Where admission has gone up once in 5 years. See animals not seen in the zoo. Pet the baby pigs. See Rattlesnakes, prairie dogs, russian wild boar, mouflon sheep, ducks, jack rabbits, 7 breeds of pheasants, 7 breeds of quail, bobcats, skunks, badgers, deer, rabbits that weigh 20 lbs., and many more. A childs delight, they can feed the animals. Long horns, rattlesnake jewelry, Kansas souvenirs. Home of the largest Prairie Dog in the world, 8,000 lbs. and don't miss our 5 legged live cow.

DEEP ROCK CAFE, Colby, Kan. ½ Mi. N. of I-70 Interchange, on St. 25. Serving a comp. menu of delicious home-cooked food. Luncheon specials daily; variety of tender steaks dinners. Many other tasty dishes to choose from; fast & courteous service always. Banquets & special parties invited. Open from 6 a.m. to 10 p.m. every day. Other services & motels close. While in Colby see the famous (Sod Town). Your genial hosts, Marion & Kay.

BURLINGTON LIQUORS, Hiway 385 & I-70. Complete selection of wine, liquors & Beer. Plenty of parking. Drive up window for your convenience.

SLOAN'S MOTEL, Burlington, Colo. Friendship Inn. U.S. 24. 27 modern well kept units, color cable TV, A.C., phones, shower or comb. baths; heated swimming pool. AAA rated, Am. Exp., Master Chg. & Bank Ameri. Conoco accepted. Restaurants nearby. Your hosts, Harry & Darleen.

I-70 SKELLY SERVICE & CAFE, Burlington, Colo. E. Burlington Interchange off I-70. Truck stop-open 24 hrs. Serving B.L.D., short orders, steaks. Gift shop.

HUSKY CAFE, Just off Ramp of I-70. Arriba, Colo's. newest & Finest, serving a comp. menu of quality food, U.S. choice steaks, Luncheon special daily, wide selection of tasty sandwiches, homemade pies. Many other savory dishes to choose from. Your hostess Carolee Thomas. **FRONTIER MOTEL,** Just off ramp of I-70. Arriba's Brand New Motel & Husky Super Service. Motel - 10 beautiful units, all doubles, air cond., TVs, W to W carpeting, Indiv. controlled heat, plenty of parking. **HUSKY SERVICE,** complete automotive service, Diesel Fuel, open 7 days, have your car serviced while dining.

SHULL'S PIANOS & ANTIQUES - TARADO MUSEUM - SOUVENIR GIFT SHOP - PACKAGE LIQUOR STORE, Arraba, Colo. Exit No. 104 Hiway 63 Jct. Just So. of Exit. Complete line of Antiques for sale, including clocks, furn. glassware, primitives, etc., specializing in Old American Cut Glass. Torado Museum adjacent to shop. A colonial House furnished with antiques & fine arts. Open for tours, also includes coin musical instruments, autos. Open daily. Adults $1.50. Under 12 Free. Phone: 1-303-768-3468.

WORLD'S WONDER VIEW TOWER, ½ Mi. W. of Genoa, Colo. on I-70 & 24. "Believe it or not" proved by Ripley, 6 States are viewed from Tower at highest point between West & East coasts outside of the Rocky Mtns. Big collection of antiques; we sell, buy or trade. Only pictograph Museum in the U.S. Two headed calf, mammoth bones, points & bones of a 200 bison kill; guns, bottles, coins, books, rocks, arrowheads, barbwire, many other things. Don't forget the annual Stone Age Fair & Flea Market held the 2nd week each June. Open Yr. round. Ph: 303-763-2309. Your western Hosts, Mr. & Mrs. Jerry Chubbuck.

You'll love the delicious recipes created by the skilled chefs at **JB STEAK HOUSE AND LOUNGE,** West edge of Limon, Colo. Hwy. 287 & 24. Phone: 775-9996. Open 6 a.m. for breakfast, luncheon, dinner. Choose your favorites from varied & tempting menu. Feat. delicious charbroiled steaks. Enjoy your favorite cocktails & after dinner drinks. Your hosts, John & Barbara O'Dwyer.

WEST LIMON MOTEL, Limon, Colo. A **Delightful Place to Stop.** 3 blks. W. of stoplite. Clean, comfortable units with air cond. & cable TVs, shaded lawn & childrens play area. Truck & Trailer parking. Excellent Restaurant close. Ph. (303) 775-9747. Your genial hosts, Rosemary & John Stockwell.

"THANK YOU FOR YOUR PATRONAGE"
PLEASE DRIVE CAREFULLY

RAMBLE MANIFESTO

From the second I wake, the pull is strong. My soul once again demands motion. I've slept in the same bed every night for nine weeks or so, about sixty sleeps in all. It's time to go.

At some point in recent memory I was just as ready for home as I am now ready for the road. Before this homebound stint, I'd been on the road for the better part of two months, driving from the West Texas badlands to the Rockies to Venice Beach, California. Cut to the present: I've only ventured more than fifty miles from home a couple of times in the sixty days since.

All of that stability adds up. I've been sitting too still for too long. The coffee isn't helping quell my nomadic impulses to be sure, instead fueling the restlessness building in the pit of my gut. Day after day, the feeling has gotten stronger and stronger and by now I've convinced myself the only cure is the road. Regardless of my diagnostic accuracy, I go through the rituals of preparation. I pack a bag of clothes, a smaller bag of toiletries, a backpack, a camera bag, and assorted other bags of various sizes.

I get up early. I load my car. I fill my travel mug with coffee. I double-check everything. I say goodbye to the house and leave a key under the mat.

Then I go. After a passing thought regarding the position of the coffeemaker's power switch, I recline into my new role. Roles, actually: driver, traveler, nomad. A man going on a journey, a stranger coming to town.

That first morning, that's the road trip big bang where it all begins. What happened before departure is no longer relevant. Home and bills and jobs and everything else in the rear-view mirror can wait. There is no better diversion from reality than the road.

Home is yin to the road's yang. The conceptual schism between the two is akin to that of the mind's left and right hemispheres, or that of order and chaos. You can't have one without the other. Home is static, stable, and studied—I know most every corner and get more intimate with the place as the clock ticks ahead. Surprises are few, but comforts are many. But you can get too comfortable. Such is the hazard of home.

The road, conversely, is impossible to know like home. Each bend holds the promise of the new, the unique, the unknown. Habit and routine take a backseat to the buzz of discovery, as mile markers and thoughts of all kinds punctuate the long distances driven.

You can get too precise in your daily routine. You can only gargle your name-brand mouthwash for exactly sixty seconds so many times before you want to kick the day-to-day to the curb. Waking leads to coffee leads to work to lunch to a workout or a daily application of facial cleanser or TV programming or prescription medication. Routine overwhelms everything else; you can actually feel habits cementing into timeworn modes of thought and existence that will be nearly impossible to change. Which brings us back to the relative chaos of the road. The opiate of perpetual motion can salve a soul.

It might sound like I want to take a vacation from myself. It's not entirely untrue. Then there is also the thought that external motion can provoke internal discovery. Life is a journey, and the road trip is a microcosmic symbol of the mortal trek toward enlightenment. Whatever.

My personal angle stems from the desire for a superlative freedom, for those intangible sensations that start in my guts and oscillate along the very center of my being. It's hard to get such primeval juices flowing from the comfort of a sofa, the gentle refrains of TV ads selling your soul into submission. But that's where these words are spilling out of my pen—a cozy dining table in a living room—as my right leg twitches, the rubber on the tip of my tennis shoe squeaking softly on the hardwood. Sure, home is nice. Home is where the heart is. Home sweet home. There's no place like home.

But there's no place like the road either. The predictability of home ultimately fuels the urge to roam. Then there's that burning desire to simply move. There's an allure to velocity that only velocity can placate.

There is nothing in life quite like cruising into a classic Western landscape, radio all the way up, windows all the way down, the sunshine and the beauty and the velocity! Velocity is all-important. Without movement the road ceases to be. Velocity is the road.

The road calls, and I must listen. And why not? It beats sitting around at home all to hell.

The American road is an endless strip of neon-lit blacktop, lined with billboards, cactus, mountains, urban sprawl, toxic waste, and open space at once desolate and inspiring and lonely and alive.

The road is also a temporary, ephemeral place. It pulses with activity with or without me, as life stories zoom by at eighty miles an hour. Motion is the norm; to move is to exist. The lack of motion is met with puzzlement and suspicion. Stopping is not a legitimate option.

I drive for hours in a meditative state. Then I think, "Well, I wonder what's it like to live here?" At some point I realized that just about every last spot on the planet was home to somebody. It's the same old shit to somebody. What exactly the same old shit is depends on geography, but it is everywhere.

Except the road. Those fleeting periods of velocity are some of the purest feelings of freedom available. The road is just the place to get lost. And in my mind that's a good thing.

Caffeine and long-distance driving are inseparable to me. Without coffee it's doubtful I'd make it very far, mentally or physically. A cup of joe is the ignition for my imagination and inspiration.

I typically refill my travel mug every time I stop. If I chug sixteen ounces of coffee per tank of gas there is very little chance I'll snooze. Between the caffeine and the sheer volume of fluid, my mind and bladder work hand in hand to keep me awake.

Another essential: music. Beauty is in the ear of the beholder, but the first rule of the road is that you can never have too much music. On a 5,000-mile journey you could easily listen to 100 different albums and not repeat once. For those types of trips, a serious library is required. Or a well-stocked iPod.

I don't want to dawdle, but I don't want to rush either. Roadside motels are fine en route, but there better be something better at the end of the line. Greasy spoons provide sustenance, but it's best to have sandwich supplies and a steady stream of hot coffee.

Habit can evolve into a near-science. Then I beg for a change, the phone to ring, an email to arrive, anything…

But nothing happens. And it won't, not unless I can will it so. And the confines of routine cannot involve driving halfway across the country, unless you drive a large vehicle for a living. To make it happen, I must go.

But the wise traveler prepares. There are certain necessities. Clothes, and an organizational system for clean clothes, dirty clothes, and those clothes in between. That usually involves a large mothership bag that remains in the trunk, a satellite bag to bring toiletries and a change into motel rooms and friends' places, and a third bag for the stuff that's in need of a wash.

A full array of camping equipment is another must-have, to shave the lodging costs down and give opportunity to park the car and venture into the woods for a day or three.

Then there's the cooler, which sits in the back seat and occasionally hosts soft drinks and sandwich ingredients. Ice is kept to a minimum.

There's a backpack filled with books and notepads and pens and the like in the front seat, as well as an assortment of compact discs with jazz, punk, and country songs. There's a laptop and a camera in the back.

Then there are the little things that suit one's tastes,: maybe breath mints, drinking water, and marijuana…just don't get caught in the red states.

If you leave at the crack of dawn it is an incredible feeling to rub your eyes at 9 a.m. and realize you are nearly 300 miles from home. It would take the pioneers weeks to make it this far. St. Louis to San Francisco was once a harrowing four-month journey. Today it's easy enough to do it in two days.

California. The geographic end of the road, unless you want to park in the Pacific, and the cultural end of the road, in terms of what people are willing to do. Mass-produced mularkey and silicone microchips pour out of the Golden State (along with oranges and cheese and a lot of other things). If the computers start thinking on their own, they'll quickly realize that Hollywood is pushing many of us humans to not think on our own. Thus is the conundrum.

APPENDIX: INFO, ETC.

STATE

Colorado Tourism Office
800-COLORADO
www.colorado.com

MAJOR CONVENTION AND VISITOR BUREAUS AND CHAMBERS OF COMMERCE

Denver Metro CVB
303-892-1112
www.denver.org

Boulder CVB
800-444-0447
www.bouldercoloradousa.com

Colorado Springs CVB
877-745-3773
www.experiencecoloradosprings.com

Durango Area Tourism Office
800-525-8855
www.durango.org

Vail Valley Tourism Bureau
970-476-1000
www.visitvailvalley.com

Breckenridge Resort Chamber
970-453-2913
www.gobreck.com

Aspen Chamber of Commerce
970-925-1940
www.aspenchamber.org

Telluride Tourism Board
888-605-2578
www.visittelluride.com

Fort Collins CVB
800-274-3678
www.ftcollins.com

Grand Junction VCB
800-962-2547
www.visitgrandjunction.com

Gunnison-Crested Butte Tourism Association
800-814-7988
www.gunnisoncrestedbutte.com

Winter Park-Fraser Valley Chamber of Commerce
800-903-7275
www.winterpark-info.com

ORGANIZATIONS

Colorado Brewers Guild
303-507-7664
www.coloradobeer.org

Colorado Lodging Association
303-297-8335
www.coloradolodging.com

Colorado River Outfitters Association
www.croa.org

Colorado Ski Country USA
3303-837-0793 (303-825-7669 for the snow report)
www.coloradoski.com

Colorado State Parks
303-866-3437
www.parks.state.co.us

Colorado Trail Foundation
303-384-3729
www.coloradotrail.org

**Association of Brewers
(Great American Beer Festival)**
303-447-0816
www.beertown.org

TRANSPORTATION

**Colorado Department of
Transportation Traveler Information**
303-639-1111
www.cotrip.org

Denver International Airport
303-342-2000
www.flydenver.com

**Regional Transportation District
(RTD)**
(Denver-area buses and light rail)
303-299-6000
www.rtd-denver.com

NATIONAL PARKS
AND MONUMENTS

**Canyon of the Ancients National
Monument**
3 miles west of Dolores
970-882-5600
www.blm.gov

Colorado National Monument
Between Fruita and Grand Junction
970-858-3617
www.nps.gov/conm

Dinosaur National Monument
Near Dinosaur
970-374-3000
www.nps.gov/dino

**Great Sand Dunes National Park
and Preserve**
East of Mosca
719-378-6300
www.nps.gov/grsa

Hovenweep National Monument
North of Cortez
970-562-4282
www.nps.gov/hove

**Black Canyon of the Gunnison
National Park**
East of Montrose
970-641-2337
www.nps.gov/blca

Rocky Mountain National Park
Between Estes Park and
Grand Lake
970-586-1206
www.nps.gov/romo

Yucca House National Monument
Between Towaoc and Cortez
970-529-4465
www.nps.gov/yuho

INDEX